NEW JERSEY COUNTRY HOUSES

THE
SOMERSET
HILLS

NEW JERSEY COUNTRY HOUSES

THE SOMERSET HILLS

VOLUME I

John K. Turpin and W. Barry Thomson

Introduction by Mark Alan Hewitt

Edited by Brooke Hyde Goode

To Carol, with
fond best wishes.

Barry

December 2004

Mountain Colony Press

Published by Mountain Colony Press, Inc.
P.O. Box 100
Far Hills, New Jersey 07931
www.mountaincolonypress.com

Copyright © 2004, John K. Turpin and W. Barry Thomson

Library of Congress Control Number: 2004103368

ISBN 0-9749504-0-8

Book design by Thomas Whitridge, Ink, Inc.,
and Antony Drobinski, Emsworth Design, Inc.
Set in Requiem type.

Printed in Italy.

We dedicate this book to the hundreds of people who, from the 1870s to World War II, commissioned, designed, built, and worked on these great country estates and, in so doing, helped create and maintain a wondrous and special world that remains an essential aspect of the cultural landscape of the Somerset Hills.

The photographs on the opposite page and the town-divider pages portray some of the landmark buildings and activities that, along with the great country houses, came to characterize the golden era of the Somerset Hills. These buildings and activities are described in the Appendix, beginning on page 237.

ARRIVAL OF 5 P. M. TRAIN, BERNARDSVILLE, N. J.

WHILE WE WAITED, the limousines—Locomobiles, Pierce-Arrows, Cadillacs, Panhards—would carry the owners of estates farther up the mountain down to the train known as the Millionaire's Express. Frequently, when the bus got down into town, we would see, coming down from the other side of the mountain, a glass-enclosed light carriage drawn by two high-stepping chestnuts, with coachman and footman on the box, moving like a procession to meet the same train. The carriage gleamed, the horses gleamed, the harness gleamed, and the tall-hatted, uniformed men sat imperturbably on the box, the coachman holding the reins precisely and the footman sitting erect, arms folded across his chest.

So it went, in a world of grass and trees and blossoms and snow. All the world was a golden quietness, and the long, bright, scented years passed, and then a man died, the kennel was disbanded, and I grew older in other places. I moved out upon the world, and the world moved in upon me, and it was as I had known it would be, for never again was the world to be quite so bright, so fair, so enchanted.

Excerpted from, "The View From the Middle," an article by Norman Hankinson that appeared in the September 12, 1964, issue of The New Yorker. *Hankinson's father was the kennel manager on the Francis G. Lloyd estate in Bernardsville—The Maples—from 1916 to 1921.*

CONTENTS

PREFACE

I N RECENT YEARS, an increasing number of well-researched and beautifully illustrated books have appeared showcasing such legendary American residential enclaves as Greenwich, Newport, Palm Beach, Beverly Hills, the Main Line outside Philadelphia, Lake Forest, and Long Island's North Shore. Somewhat surprisingly, but much to our gratification, no such full-scale effort has been undertaken for New Jersey's Somerset Hills in nearly a century.

For more than twenty years a growing collection of professional photographs and archival images depicting interiors and exteriors of some of the finest estates in the area have been accumulating in our files. As each year passed and the collection grew larger, the desire became stronger to share this treasure trove in the form of a large full-color book. In the fall of 2000 the decision was made to proceed. What started out, however, to be a handsome picture book with abbreviated text and captions, was transformed over the next three years into an extensively researched effort to identify and bring to life the architects and the patrons who commissioned them to design the extraordinary country houses that were built during the "golden age" of the Somerset Hills, the period from the 1870s through the Great Depression. While a great deal of interesting new information was unearthed about the people who designed and built these great estates, so too were some ingrained myths and local lore debunked. In several instances, it was discovered that long-held beliefs that particular houses were designed by certain well-known architects were completely erroneous. On the other hand, it became clear just how many estates *had* been designed by some of the most prominent architects and landscape architects in America. As the reams of biographical information grew, it also became clear that the Bernardsville mountain and the surrounding area had been home to some of the most accomplished and noteworthy people of the era, including financiers, inventors, attorneys, industrialists, and architects.

As the project grew in scope so did the length of the book, as additional historical text and period photographs, maps, and architectural drawings were added to the mix. To include all the images and text we had assembled would have made the book unwieldy, yet to engage in the wholesale elimination of such matter would have been unthinkable. In the period covered—from shortly after the Civil War, when many great fortunes were being amassed, to the end of the Great Depression and the eve of World War II—there was a break in estate construction during World War I. So, the decision was made to divide the work into two volumes. Volume I generally covers the period from the 1870s to 1918, while Volume II will look at the prolific estate-building activity between the end of the First World War and 1940, including a surprising number of houses that were constructed during the Great Depression. Volume II will also include biographies of the architects and landscape architects whose work is represented in the Somerset Hills, as well as a complete index and bibliography covering both volumes.

An initial list of estate properties in the area revealed a larger number than originally anticipated. Many of these properties were exquisitely gentrified and enlarged farmhouses. With a few exceptions, we decided that those houses would make good grist for another book and that we would concentrate primarily on the grand mansions that were originally constructed as such.

Remarkably, unlike some other estate enclaves that have had their architectural heritage mercilessly bulldozed to make way for faceless, uninspired development, a surprising number of the grand estate residences that were built in the Somerset Hills during the period covered by these volumes remain standing today. In fact, more than a score of them are over 100 years old, and most are in very good condition and still serving their original purpose as residences. Of the relatively small number lost—some of which are included in these volumes—all but a few were claimed by fire, and most of those were promptly rebuilt. Although a number of estates have not retained their original acreage, a surprising number have. Most of the others have kept enough surrounding property to maintain an appropriate air of their original elegance. Some have been converted to golf clubs, convents, or schools.

There has been a renaissance of sorts in recent years as new owners have recognized the gratification to be had by restoring and living in these historic estate residences.

In fact, several of the properties that had been converted along the way to institutional uses have since been returned to private ownership.

In the pages that follow, you are invited to savor the visual pleasures of the houses and gardens that were designed by some of America's greatest architects and landscape architects. We are privileged to live in an area that retains so much of their work intact. Certainly, the towns of the Somerset Hills have changed and grown more densely populated, and will continue to do so. The communities have been able to weather the intrusion of two interstate highways and subsequent heavy development, particularly in the Pluckemin–Bedminster corridor. Ever-increasing traffic has put our once-sleepy highways and byways to the test. And yet, from the Bernardsville mountain to the open, rolling fields of Bedminster, the communities of the Somerset Hills have, for the most part, retained much of their character, despite these significant external pressures.

It is our wish, above all others, that the publication of *New Jersey Country Houses: The Somerset Hills* will lead to a heightened awareness of our special heritage and the need to be ever-vigilant in its preservation.

John K. Turpin   W. Barry Thomson

INTRODUCTION

During the last quarter of the nineteenth century, American culture was rife with nostalgic paens to rural life. Donald G. Mitchell, the author of *Rural Studies, with Hints for Country Places* (1867), advised his urban readers to buy an old farm and build on it a country house, where they could recapture something of a rapidly vanishing way of life, even as they acquired vast sums of excess capital in business ventures that even today seem miraculous in their plenitude. America's richest families from this era began to purchase landscapes that evoked the most romantic myths of country living and leisure. The Hudson Valley, Mount Desert Island, Long Island, and the Adirondack Mountains were among the first to capture their imagination. No longer valuable merely as geological or agricultural resources, rural landscapes became a symbol of gentility and wealth. One of the earliest, and most beautiful, of these mythic places was the Upper Raritan River Valley of New Jersey, now known as the Somerset Hills.

The pages that follow chronicle in rich detail the country houses and gardens built in this unique place during an era that seems quite distant from contemporary America. Jack Turpin and Barry Thomson grew up in the Somerset Hills, and watched the society and the land change with each passing decade, but never relinquished their own romance with the golden age of the country estates that were hidden there. Their passion for the architecture, people, and landscapes of this corner of New Jersey is alive in every photograph and every word in this marvelous book.

Proximate to New York City and Philadelphia, the Upper Raritan Valley drew summer cottagers during the mid-1800s, but did not acquire a society cachet until the late 1880s. It was then that a select group of wealthy families from both New Jersey and New York began to colonize the area around Morristown, spreading their houses southward toward Bernardsville and what are now Peapack-Gladstone, Far Hills, and Bedminster as land became more scarce. John F. Dryden (1839–1911), a founder of the Prudential Insurance Company, helped lead the way in 1899 with his massive mansion, *Stronghold*. Dryden served in the United States Senate from 1902 to 1907, and was a dominant figure in both society and politics in New Jersey for two decades. The senator did not build his George B. Post-designed house, but he remodeled it in his own image, drawing on its geomorphic, fortresslike character and echoing the massive stonework of Post's extraordinary headquarters building for the Prudential in Newark. George I. Seney fueled interest in the Somerset Hills by underwriting a large resort hotel in Bernardsville, soon to be home to a "mountain colony" of wealthy summer residents from New York and Newark. By 1895 the hills between Somerville and Morristown were dotted with country houses, many supporting farms and equestrian complexes.

As one reviews the eclectic array of houses and gardens built between the 1870s and through the Great Depression, one is struck not merely by the architecture but by the visions and lives of the extraordinary patrons that came to the area in search of a respite from their hectic professional lives. Dryden and his compatriots were blazing trails in many areas of commerce and politics, as the fascinating portraits of each owner and house make clear. They represent a cross section of the most celebrated men and women in the New York area during the Progressive Era. The Roebling and Stevens families were engineering pioneers. Ledyard Blair and his father and grandfather financed railroads. John H. Ballantine made a fortune on his popular ale. Charles Engelhard Sr. came to dominate the precious metals industry and was an adviser to President Franklin Roosevelt. Richard Lindabury made his reputation as a bulldog litigator, but enjoyed his *Meadow Brook Farm* as a place to breed fine Holsteins and Guernseys for the county fair. Haley Fiske presided over the massive Metropolitan Life Insurance Company. Many were attracted to the area for its association with equestrian pursuits, such as foxhunting, steeplechase, coaching, polo, and dressage.

The colony formed itself around the Essex Hunt and the Somerset Hills Country Club. James Cox Brady's 5,000-acre *Hamilton Farm* became the center of riding and hunting activities with its state-of-the-art facilities for horses of all breeds. Brady and Charles Pfizer, of the pharmaceutical empire, vied with each other for top breeding honors, with their thoroughbreds, Hackney ponies, hunters, Clydesdales and Percheron draft horses. Brady's stable was constructed in 1916 at a cost of $250,000, and was the largest in the country at that time. At *Yademos* in Bernardsville and at his farms in what are now Peapack-Gladstone, Bedminster, and Chester, Pfizer maintained the hunters and hounds of the Essex Hunt, which he had moved from its former home in Montclair. Several generations of the plutocracy came to enjoy the pleasures of foxhunting here, including former first lady Jacqueline Kennedy Onassis.

Golfers delighted in the beautiful mountaintop venues cut by the North Branch of the Raritan River and its tributary streams. Like most upper class colonies, the cachet of exclusivity lured many prominent families to the Somerset Hills. And with these fortunes came an entire population of servants and merchants to maintain the estate lifestyle. Bernardsville's population rose in the early twentieth century due to the influx of Italian, German, Irish, and East European immigrants who worked in the mansions on the mountain above the village. Farmers from many of the local communities were employed to run the agricultural enterprises on the estates. A small resort enclave even developed in the tiny hamlet of Pottersville, as summer visitors from the cities came to enjoy the same views as the wealthy.

The greatest artistic product of this social phenomenon was the architecture and gardens of this New Jersey arcadia. Here, too, the most prominent and talented professionals were drawn to ply their skills. First among the architects of the colony was George B. Post, a founding member who resided in his own country house, *Claremont*, until his death in 1913. Barry Thomson has shown that Post and his sons designed from scratch or altered over two dozen houses in the Somerset Hills, including *Boulderwood*, *Malvern*, and *Appletrees*. Three of his four sons, George Jr., William, and Wright, also resided in the Post family enclave on the Bernardsville mountain, and daughter Alice and her husband, Arthur Turnbull, resided in nearby Far Hills. We are fortunate to have a well-preserved group of domestic commissions from this superb American architect and his sons extant today.

Another faithful resident was Henry Janeway Hard-

enbergh, the New Jersey-born architect of many of the era's finest hotels, including the Plaza in New York, Willard in Washington, and Copley-Plaza in Boston. He relished life at his estate, *Renemede*, and supported the Bernardsville community by donating the designs for the parish house of St. Bernard's Church and the town's first high school. Hardenbergh also collaborated with Boston architect Guy Lowell in creating the *Natirar* estate for Walter and Kate Macy Ladd in Peapack. James Leal Greenleaf, a prominent landscape architect, was also a New Jersey resident who cut his teeth on several important commissions in the area, the largest of which were *Blairsden* in Peapack and the James B. Duke estate gardens in Somerville. A local landscape architect, John Rowlett Brinley, from Morristown, is credited with nearly twenty commissions for estates in the Somerset Hills, and many more in New Vernon, Morristown, Madison, and beyond.

As might be expected, many of the nation's finest architects and garden designers found employment here. Carrère & Hastings, designers of the New York Public Library, designed *Blairsden,* one of the greatest house and garden ensembles of the Beaux-Arts era. Their protégés, Delano & Aldrich, are represented by several fine houses in the area, while Harrie T. Lindeberg catered to patrons in the Morristown area, such as Seth Thomas Jr. and Paul Moore. Local talents A. Musgrave Hyde and Eugene Mason used their family connections to win commissions. Larger New York firms, such as Cross & Cross, Hiss & Weekes, and John Russell Pope, also designed fine residences for New Jersey patrons. The house Pope designed in Far Hills for Thomas Frothingham, and later occupied by the John Sloane family, is now home to the United States Golf Association. The Olmsted Brothers, Ellen Shipman, and other fine landscape architects helped plan elaborate gardens on the larger estates. One of the most successful designers of country houses after 1925 was Mott B. Schmidt, who worked for the Dillon, Fowler, and Cowperthwaite families well into the 1950s. The Cowperthwaite farm has lately been prominent as the home of John DeLorean and most recently as the Trump National Golf Club.

Despite New Jersey's alarming rate of land development during the last fifty years, much of the beautiful landscape comprising the Somerset Hills estates remains intact. Newly wealthy patrons have purchased many houses and restored them to their past grandeur. Others have been destroyed or altered beyond recognition. Turpin and Thomson's monumental effort to document the history of these unique American places will help to preserve more of this landscape by educating new residents to the value of their heritage. Preservation efforts, such as the recent acquisition of *Natirar* by Somerset County, will benefit from a greater sensitivity to the architecture and gardens of this golden era of country house building in America. The beautiful photographs in this volume make an unassailable case for the value of the great estates, no less as social documents than as artistic statements of their time and place. The detailed text gives the reader a vivid context for appreciating their impact on American culture. The book's graphic design reminds us of the elegance and grace of a bygone era. As a whole, *New Jersey Country Houses: The Somerset Hills*, presents a marvelous and compelling chronicle of country life in one of America's most storied environments.

Mark Alan Hewitt

PROLOGUE

AMERICANS HAVE LONG VALUED and pursued the arcadian ideal of the bucolic life. The gentility of social life in the country and the healthful attributes and physical beauty of nature have long been contrasted with the many perceived social ills and the congestion and blight of urban centers. The allure of country life was particularly strong during the period of great urban, industrial, and economic growth that occurred in the decades following the Civil War. This was a period characterized by dramatic social shifts. On the one hand, there were huge waves of immigration from overseas and domestic migration to the increasingly crowded and noisome northern cities. At the same time, the nation witnessed the accumulation of immense wealth by a select, but growing and increasingly interrelated, group of plutocrats eager and determined to join the ranks of the upper class. As the sociologist E. Digby Baltzell—who coined the acronym WASP—has noted in his book, *Protestant Establishment: Aristocracy and Caste in America* (1964), citing the work of historian Richard Hofstadter, between 1870 and 1900 the nation's wealth more than quadrupled from $30.4 billion to $126.7 billion, and doubled again by 1914 to nearly $254.2 billion. Yet fifty percent of this wealth in 1910 was controlled by less than one percent of the population, a group consisting of only about 40,000 families.

These new moguls, in an effort to assimilate themselves into the established upper class, lavishly spent their newfound wealth to acquire the physical manifestations of the aristocratic life: large city houses and country estates, artwork from Europe, Paris couture, and elegant toys such as carriages, yachts, and private railroad cars. Once ensconced at the apex of society, they established new institutions and social conventions, often copied from European models, to ensure their social control and the exclusivity of their caste, as well as to reinforce the symbolic bulwarks between themselves and the rest of society. These new or imitated social creations included the country club, the urban social club, the Social Register, ancestral associations, artistic and cultural organizations, and recreational activities that were limited, as a practical matter, to those with the money and time to pursue them, such as yachting, coaching, foxhunting, and polo.

One of the most important means by which these new magnates showcased their wealth and established and maintained their credentials among the social elite was by building large country houses for seasonal occupancy in one or more of country's exclusive resort "colonies," such as Newport, Rhode Island; Bar Harbor, Maine; Lenox, Massachusetts; the Main Line outside Philadelphia; the Hudson River Valley of New York; Aiken, South Carolina—and the Somerset Hills of New Jersey. These estates, including many in this volume, were often virtually self-supporting enterprises on vast acreage, providing every creature comfort and recreational activity imaginable, as well as a steady supply of agricultural products for the owner's country and city houses. Although these country properties afforded great privacy and self-sufficiency, they were not intended to be a means of retreat from society. Almost invariably, they were established in proximity to other estates, to exclusive country clubs, or to cities that provided the financial wherewithal by which the entire confection was built and sustained. Above all, the great country estate was intended to be an example of conspicuous consumption, the pursuit of leisure, and a blatant statement of the owner's social standing.

At their zenith in the 1920s and 1930s, the estates of the Somerset Hills stretched in an almost unbroken quilt of contiguous properties—broken only by the several town centers—across a nearly 100-square-mile area taking in parts of Somerset and Morris counties. These properties, which ranged in size from as few as 10 to as many as 5,000 acres, had an impact on the cultural landscape of the area that was more profound and lasting than any other single phenomenon since European settlers first set foot in the region.

Although the communities that came to be identified as the Somerset Hills were only thirty miles from Newark and forty miles from New York, until the 1870s and 1880s the area grew slowly and independently of—and largely oblivious to—the outside world that lay beyond a horseback or wagon ride to the county seats of Somerville or Morristown. Until the railroad arrived in Bernardsville in 1872 and in Gladstone in 1890, the most significant disruptions to the quiet patterns and pace of life, and the relative remoteness of the area, were the periodic transits of soldiers during the American Revolution.

The elegant estates that seemed to sprout on each hillock during the latter years of the nineteenth and first decades of the twentieth centuries fundamentally changed the cultural, economic, and social make-up, as well as the physical landscape, of the area.

Although to some extent local residents carried on as they had before the emergence of the mountain colony, ultimately, almost no one could escape the collective effect of the arrival of the wealthy "cottagers." Many of those who sold their family farms to the plutocrats from New York and Newark wound up helping to build the new estates and remained as employees; and local contractors went from building vernacular barns and gristmills to constructing large and luxurious mansions and coach barns designed by some of the country's most prominent architects.

The once-homogeneous population was further changed by an infusion of new people, from the Italian masons who came to build the railroad and construct many of the mansions and new roads, to Irish maids and groomsmen and English butlers. New organizations and institutions also evolved. Some, such as the Essex Hunt, the Somerset Hills Country Club, and the Somerset Bridle Path Association, were designed exclusively to serve the needs of the denizens of the mountain colony. Other institutions, such as public libraries, the fall agricultural fairs, new public schools and churches, and the visiting nurse association, though often heavily supported by the new arrivals, enhanced the life of the broader community.

Many of the prominent new residents took an active interest in their communities, donating time, service, and money. Many served in local government, on the boards of local institutions, or on private organizations that supported the work of government.

The estates and farms of the wealthy became the most significant economic engines for each of the towns in the area. Many of the estates were, by far, the largest direct employers in their communities; and, indirectly, these grand enterprises helped create and spur the growth of many local businesses, many still in existence, that supplied the estates with products and services.

The physical appearance of the region was also profoundly changed as a result of these estates. New roads were laid out and improved, very often underwritten by the wealthy residents. Hundreds of new trees, often huge full-grown specimens, were planted on the estates and along public roads to landscape what had been a largely open, field-covered terrain. Beautiful stone walls, gates, bridges, and dams were constructed, and new town parks and recreational fields were developed, often donated or spearheaded by residents of the mountain colony.

Although most of the people who commissioned, designed, built, and worked on these great estates have passed from the scene, we are fortunate that, despite the enormous growth that has taken place since World War II, so much of what they created has remained as an architectural and cultural legacy. It is our hope that the following pages will provide the reader with at least a glimpse, and a somewhat better understanding, of that legacy and of a period that transformed the Somerset Hills.

BERNARDSVILLE

The Somerset Inn.

The raised third floor, classical cornice, and columned porches are believed to have been added after George I. Seney's death in 1893.

THE MAPLES

THE BERNARDSVILLE estate known as *The Maples* was home to two prominent citizens, each of whom has a town street named in his honor: George Ingraham Seney (1826–1893), president of the Metropolitan Bank of New York and the man partly credited with popularizing the area as a summer retreat for wealthy New Yorkers in the late 1800s; and Francis Guerin Lloyd (1848–1920), president of the haberdashery Brooks Brothers.

The estate's centerpiece was a stately red-brick mansion flanked by tall white columns. The date of construction is unknown, but reports suggest that its original section may date back to the early 1800s. Francis Peppard Jr., a minister's son, married Clarissa Savidge, and the couple built a large brick house and other estate buildings on a piece of land bordered by what are now Mendham, Lloyd, and Washington Corner roads. One of the Peppards' sons, Reuben Clark, inherited the house after his father's death in 1840. He remained there until his own death in 1862. His widow, Catherine, stayed on until 1869, when she sold the house and about fifty surrounding acres to Francis Oliver, who ran several boarding houses in the area.

In 1871 the property was bought by George I. Seney, the banker and philanthropist who did as much to build the fame of Bernardsville's mountain colony as any man of his era. Seney most likely added on to the existing Peppard home, since the original structure was never known to have been demolished. In the early 1870s, on the nearby site of what had been the Oliver boarding house on Mendham Road, Seney built the Highland Hotel, later renamed the Somerset Inn, a luxurious resort, with accommodation for 400 guests, that enticed prosperous residents of New York and Newark to visit the area, buy land, and build their own summer "cottages."

Seney came from a prominent family whose ancestors included the first commodore of the United States Navy and members of the Continental Congress and first United States Congress. He was well known as a philanthropist and art collector, donating money and paintings gener-ously to schools, hospitals, and museums, including the Metropolitan Museum of Art. He suffered a reversal of fortune when defaults on railroad loans forced the failure of the Metropolitan Bank in 1884. To maintain solvency and ensure that depositors were paid, Seney auctioned large parts of his extensive art collection in what were said to be the largest art sales in the United States at that time.

After Seney's death, his 1,000-acre estate was sold to the Somerset Land Company, which had been organized by Seney's son, Robert, to develop the property and manage the Somerset Inn. In 1898 the company, which was then managed by brothers Grant and Evander Schley, sold the former Seney residence and fifty acres to Francis G. Lloyd, the guiding genius behind the success of Brooks Brothers for more than half a century.

Lloyd began working at Brooks Brothers in 1862 as a helper in the military-clothing department, which was very busy due to the Civil War. He rose to become the firm's president in 1903, serving in that capacity until his death in 1920. Apart from golf, Lloyd's passion was his prizewinning Scottish terriers, which were kept at the Walescott Kennels on his estate, which he named *The Maples*. He was devoted to his Scotties and on weekends would take up to thirty at a time out for a run. He was not in the least interested in selling his beloved dogs but would give one to a visitor to whom he took a liking. Lloyd was also an art connoisseur and owned one of the largest private collections of Japanese prints in America.

The house was demolished in early 2004.

Second Empire-style frame house occupied by the George I. Seney family.

YADEMOS

YADEMOS has seen several owners since its construction on the Bernardsville mountain in 1881, but it is best known as the home of Charles Pfizer (1861–1929), son of the founder of the pharmaceutical firm that bears the family name. Locally, Pfizer is remembered as the man who brought the Essex Hunt to the Somerset Hills.

Yademos—"someday" spelled backward—was built by George I. Seney, who helped popularize Bernardsville in the late 1800s as a summer retreat for leaders of industry and finance. President of the Metropolitan Bank of New York, Seney hired the architectural firm of Lamb & Rich to design the stone-and-shingle house for his son, Robert. Although Lamb & Rich designed many types of structures, including buildings at Barnard, Smith, Dartmouth, and Colgate colleges, they are best remembered for their shingled residential commissions of the 1880s, including *Sagamore Hill*, the Oyster Bay, Long Island, country home of Theodore Roosevelt.

In the early 1890s the estate was acquired by Pfizer. He bought all of the hounds, horses, and equipment of the Essex County Hunt, which had been established two decades earlier at the Essex County Country Club in Montclair, and relocated them to kennels on Seney's estate, adjacent to *Yademos*. The following summer, he bought a 200-acre farm in Gladstone, converted the barns into stables and kennels, and there established the headquarters of the newly named Essex Hunt.

An avid horseman who devoted his life to foxhunting and other equestrian pursuits, both in the United States and Europe, Pfizer served as master—and sole owner—of the Essex Hunt for more than twenty years. He took a personal interest in all aspects of the running of the kennels and stables, and paid all expenses, refusing to accept any subscriptions. Pfizer was renowned for his sportsmanship, generosity, and hospitality. In 1899 he organized the area's first polo club at Bernardsville, and in 1910 he initiated an annual race meeting luncheon in honor of the farmers over whose land the hunt rode. Originally known as Farmer's Day, the annual event continues to this day, with landowners feted by a pig roast or cocktail party. In 1912 Pfizer met with severe financial losses and turned the hunt over to a committee that formed the Essex Fox Hounds.

Pfizer created exquisite Japanese gardens at *Yademos*, which became part of movie history when, in 1915, the estate—along with Grant Schley's *Froh Heim*—was selected as the location for the filming of *Madame Butterfly*. The star, Mary Pickford, who played the eponymous Japanese geisha, and her actor husband, Douglas Fairbanks, reportedly spent many hours relaxing on the tennis court at *Yademos*.

In more recent years, *Yademos* has served as the backdrop for a Lincoln Continental advertisement and has been the site of a fund-raising house tour. Among the outstanding features of the mansion's interior are an elaborate wickerwork balustrade and a recessed fireplace of blue tile in the dining room.

Given its name, Yademos, *by Charles Pfizer, a subsequent owner, the house was designed by Lamb & Rich and built in 1881 for Robert Seney. The architects were well known for their Shingle-style houses, including Theodore Roosevelt's* Sagamore Hill *at Oyster Bay on Long Island.*

Japanese garden at Yademos, where scenes from actress Mary Pickford's 1915 film Madame Butterfly *were filmed.*

Sketches of interior details of the Robert Seney residence—later named Yademos by Charles Pfizer—by the architects, Lamb & Rich, that appeared in the December 3, 1881, issue of The American Architect and Building News. *The original sketches are in the Bernardsville Public Library. A sketch of the exterior appeared in the February 11, 1882, issue of the same publication.*

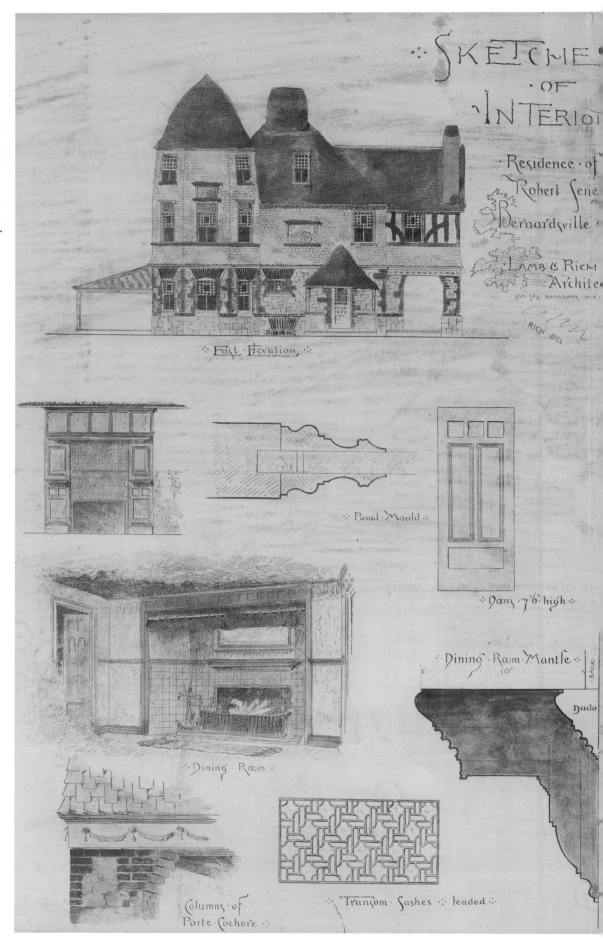

Cochere Entrance

D.N. MANTLE

Conductor

Architrave

Hall Mantle
Stone and Brick

Hall Shelf

Rail

BRICK

Hall · Balustrade · of · Wicker · work

Hall to Dining Rm

HALL
of · Hand · Floated · Plaster

CLAREMONT

G EORGE BROWNE POST (1837–1913), a founding
father of Bernardsville's mountain colony, is considered by Robert A. M. Stern, one of today's most respected
architects, to have been "one of the most prolific, prominent and professional architects in the second half of the
nineteenth century."

Although in his own lifetime Post was acknowledged
by the noted Chicago architect and city planner Daniel
Burnham as "the father of the tall building in New York,"
he and his sons designed buildings of many types. Their
commissions included everything from early skyscrapers
to banks, hospitals, churches, museums, civic and academic buildings, and country and city houses, including a
number of residences in the Somerset Hills as well as the
grandiose Cornelius Vanderbilt mansion in New York
City that once occupied the entire block between Fifty-
seventh and Fifty-eighth Streets on Fifth Avenue. Post is
perhaps best known, however, for his designs of the New
York Stock Exchange and the Wisconsin state capitol.

Post was descended from a prosperous, socially prominent, and well-connected merchant family in New York.
He was included among the first "Four Hundred" in 1892,
the group that constituted New York "society," according
to Ward McAllister, the self-appointed social arbiter of the
time. In 1858 Post earned a bachelor's degree from the
School of Civil Engineering and Architecture at the University of the City of New York (as New York University
was known at the time), then apprenticed under Richard
Morris Hunt, who had been trained at the École des
Beaux-Arts in Paris. During the Civil War he attained the
rank of colonel in the Twenty-second Regiment and thereafter was often referred to as "Colonel Post."

George Post and his family first came to Bernardsville
about 1871 on the recommendation of his cousin Edgar W.
Voris, a doctor who owned a farm on Mendham Road and
who thought the country air would be beneficial for the
health of Post's wife, Alice Matilda Stone, who suffered
from rheumatism. At first the family rented rooms at
Oliver's boarding house on Mendham Road, a property
that was later the site of the luxurious Somerset Inn.

In April 1871 Post bought the 104-acre Eliza Ballentine
farm and the 106-acre William Ballentine Jr. farm along

The first Claremont Farms *residence of the George B. Post family, originally the Ballentine family farmhouse. It was altered and enlarged several times by Post. After it was sold by Post to Anthony R. Kuser in 1903, the house was significantly renovated, including a new façade, and was renamed* Faircourt *(see pages 42–45). The house was demolished sometime after 1933.*

what is now Claremont Road (the Ballentines were not related to the Ballantine brewery family from Newark who later owned property in the same area). By the end of that year, the Posts had acquired nearly 300 acres, and they continued to purchase land in the area over succeeding years. The Ballentine farmhouse was substantially enlarged and altered by the Posts for their use, and the entire property was named *Claremont Farms*, the name taken from Post's grandfather's large estate along the Hudson River in New York City.

In 1903 Post sold the family's original home in Bernardsville to Anthony R. Kuser, and the following year set about designing and building a new home on property that he owned across Post Lane. The result was *Claremont*, a large neo-Federal-style stone-and-terra-cotta structure—one of the Post firm's most notable residential commissions—that 100 years later is still owned by the Post family. The home originally featured a Palladian-arched porte cochère at the north entrance (since removed) and a two-story curved portico on the southern, garden façade. Inside, the home's commodious first-floor rooms open off a wide center hall. A grand staircase leading from the entrance hall to the second floor once afforded sweeping views down the mountainside from the garden-side stair landing. In addition to the usual complement of stables, barns, gardener's cottage, and other outbuildings, the estate featured the family's private nine-hole golf course.

Post's earliest known residential commission in the Somerset Hills (other than alterations to the former Ballentine residence on his own property) was a towered stone villa, originally called *Crow's Foot*, near his home on Claremont Road, which he designed in 1886 for J. Coleman Drayton, a New York lawyer and son-in-law of William Astor. In 1898 John F. Dryden, a founder and third president of the Prudential Insurance Company and later a United States senator from New Jersey, acquired the Drayton home, renamed it *Stronghold*, and hired Post to alter and enlarge it.

Over the next four decades, the Somerset Hills witnessed what was and remains the greatest concentration of residential architecture produced by the firm of George B. Post & Sons, including several homes for members of the extended Post family, including: *Woodedge*, for William Stone Post, one of George Post's sons who is credited with much of the firm's design work in the area; *Kenilwood*, for another son, George B. Post Jr.; *Teviot Farm* in Far Hills, for Post's daughter, Alice, and her husband, Arthur Turnbull; *Appletrees*, for Arthur Turnbull's brother, Ramsay; *Kennil House*, for Catesby ap L. Jones and his first wife, Lilian Post Jones, a daughter of William S. Post; and *Malvern,* for Malvina Appleton, a distant relative of the Post family. In addition, the Post firm designed from scratch or altered the residences or estate buildings for twenty-five other

North façade showing the original Palladian-arched porte cochère, which was later removed. The lion sculptures remain.

clients in the area, including: Eliza Cameron Bradley, Palmer Campbell, Caroline Ellen Condict, Forrest Dryden, Charles Engelhard Sr., Mary Pyne Filley, Haley Fiske, Anthony R. Kuser, J. Dryden Kuser, William S. Lawson, Joseph Larocque, Edward A. LeRoy, Edwin A.S. Lewis, Richard V. Lindabury, Francis G. Lloyd, Clarence Blair Mitchell, Charles Moran, William Page, Percy R. Pyne, John A. Roebling II, George B. Salisbury, George C. Smith, Charles F. Squibb, Mrs. Robert L. Stevens, and Schuyler S. Wheeler.

Although church-related buildings never constituted a significant part of the Post firm's architectural practice, several examples of this aspect of the firm's work exist in the Somerset Hills, including the only church that George Post is known to have designed that was built from scratch, the 1909–10 rubble-stone Italian Evangelical Presbyterian Church on Maple Street in Bernardsville, which is now a private residence. The firm did, however, alter or enlarge several church structures in the area. The earliest such work consisted of alterations, made in 1876, to the First Presbyterian Church, known as the Hilltop Church, in Mendham. In 1903 William S. Post designed the stone parsonage for the Bernardsville Methodist Church. George Post donated the design for a half-octagon-shaped addition to the Basking Ridge Presbyterian Church, his own parish church, in 1908; and nearly fifteen

years later, in 1922, his firm designed the sexton's cottage for that church.

Other Post architectural commissions in the area include the original clubhouse, overlooking Ravine Lake, for the Somerset Hills Country Club (1897–98) and alterations to the original Bernardsville public library (1903–4). Firm records also refer to alterations to the "nurses home" in Bernardsville (1916), which is thought to be the Olcott Avenue headquarters of the Visiting Nurse Association of Somerset Hills.

George Browne Post died at *Claremont* the day after Thanksgiving in 1913. He had been an architect for about fifty-five years and had established a practice that was widely known and respected, not only for its exceptional standard of design and breadth of building types, but also for its contributions to the technology and practice of architecture. The Somerset Hills has benefited for having been called home by several generations of Post family members and for the large number of Post-designed buildings that still grace the area.

The present north façade, without the original porte cochère.
In recent years, the owners have undertaken a major restoration project,
including the rehabilitation of the terra cotta trim.

South façade of Claremont *with semicircular portico that served as a stage for the "moonlight serenade" fund-raising concerts in 1942 that featured exiled members of the Vienna Philharmonic.*

CLAREMONT has been owned and occupied by members of the Post family since it was built, except for a nearly ten-year period in the 1940s when it was owned by the Prince and Princess Chavchavadze. George Chavchavadze, a concert pianist, was a member of an old and prominent family from what is now the independent republic of Georgia. With his mother and siblings, he escaped from Russia in 1918 during the revolution, ultimately settling in London. His father was detained in Russia and was later executed under the regime of Joseph Stalin. George Chavchavadze's wealthy wife, the former Countess de Breteuil, was born Elizabeth Ridgway, the daughter of an American mother and French father.

During the time the Chavchavadzes resided at *Claremont*, the estate served as a sanctuary for a wide array of exiled Europeans, authors, musicians, and other artists, many of whom, like the Chavchavadzes, had been displaced by World War II. A cottage on the property was occupied by Colonel Ronald Victor Courtenay Bodley, a British author and close personal friend of Thomas Edward Lawrence, the famous Lawrence of Arabia. Bodley later married Harriet Moseley, a sister of Frederick Strong Moseley Jr., who built the Bedminster estate that is now Fiddler's Elbow Country Club.

Near the end of the war, the same cottage was occupied by the American composer, Aaron Copland, who had a passing acquaintance with the Chavchavadzes through New York music circles. Copland's stay at *Claremont* proved to be a productive one—he composed the orchestral suite version of his famous ballet, *Appalachian Spring*; the score for *The Cummington Story*, a documentary film that had been commissioned by the Office of War Information; and the second movement of his monumental Third Symphony. Many of Copland's friends and fellow composers were regular visitors to *Claremont*, including Leonard Bernstein, Samuel Barber, and Gian-Carlo Menotti.

The Chavchavadzes were a colorful and hospitable couple who welcomed a seemingly endless stream of people to their country estate, from the wealthy and well known, such as Mrs. William Randolph Hearst, to struggling performers, such as Yul Brynner, who was then a largely unknown Russian nightclub performer and trapeze artist. *Claremont* also hosted many exiled, well-heeled, titled Europeans, who were known somewhat disparagingly as the "St. Regis refugees," after the luxurious New York hotel where many of them waited out the war years. Even during the Chavchavadzes' periodic absences from Bernardsville, *Claremont* served as a home-away-from-home for various artists, including the Marquis de Cuevas and members of his ballet company for which Prince Chavchavadze had once composed music.

Before and during his time at *Claremont*, George Chavchavadze gave piano recitals and organized concerts around the country to raise money in support of the Allied war effort. *Claremont* served as a stage for two such concerts in 1942. Billed as "moonlight serenades," the concerts were intended to be reminiscent of the famous outdoor concerts that had been held at the Mozarteum in Salzburg before the 1938 Austrian Anschluss. The musicians at these elegant evening performances were seated on the mansion's semicircular, two-story, columned portico facing audiences of more than 900 who were seated in chairs on the lawn. The moonlit setting included what was then an unobstructed view of the lights of Manhattan in the distance. Patrons for the events included an extensive roster of local citizens, dignitaries, and other notables, including many famous personages from the worlds of the performing and fine arts. The concerts featured many prominent musicians, virtually all of whom had performed in Salzburg before the German annexation of Austria. The orchestra consisted of about thirty exiled members of the Vienna Philharmonic, and soloists included violinist Nathan Milstein, pianist Egon Petri, and flutist René Le Roy, all under the baton of Hugo Burghauser, the renowned bassoonist and former chairman and conductor of the Vienna Philharmonic.

With the end of the war, it all came to an end. In late 1945 Aaron Copland left Bernardsville, and in 1949 the Chavchavadzes sold *Claremont* back to the Post family and returned to Europe, thus ending a fascinating chapter in this great estate's long and storied history.

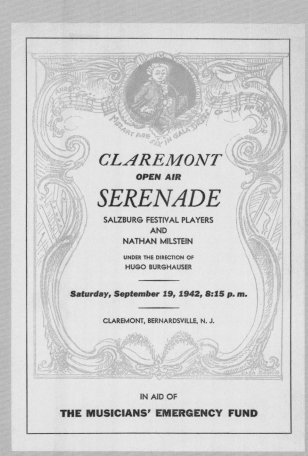

Program from the September 19, 1942, outdoor concert at Claremont *that attracted an audience of more than 900 prominent guests.*

THE MOZART FAMILY
(From the Painting by Carmontelle)

PROGRAM

NATIONAL ANTHEM

1. WATER MUSIC . . . . . . *G. F. Handel*
   Six Movements
   (Arr. by Sir Hamilton Harty)

2. SERENADE FOR STRINGS . . . . *Joseph Haydn*

3. CONCERTO IN E FLAT FOR FRENCH HORN
   AND ORCHESTRA . . . . *W. A. Mozart*
   K.-Nr. 447

TIBOR SHIK

4. FIVE MENUETS . . . . . *W. A. Mozart*
   1. The Organ Grinder
   2. Menuet in G Major
   3. The Canary
   4. Menuet in D Major
   5. The Sleigh Drive

   (Intermission—30 minutes)

5. PROMETHEUS OUVERTURE . . . *L. V. Beethoven*

6. THREE MOVEMENTS FOR VIOLIN AND
   ORCHESTRA . . . . . *W. A. Mozart*
   Rondo — Adagio — Rondo

NATHAN MILSTEIN

7. SYMPHONY NR. 35 IN D MAJOR (Haffner) . *W. A. Mozart*

Conductor
PROFESSOR HUGO BURGHAUSER

PLEASE BRING THIS PROGRAM WITH YOU

WOODEDGE

Many of the offspring of the earliest members of the Bernardsville mountain colony returned to the area after their schooling to establish their own homes. The children of the architect George B. Post and his wife, Alice, were no exception. By 1905 four of them lived in the area in houses designed by the Post firm: *Kenilwood*, *Teviot Farm*, *White Lodge*, and *Woodedge*.

Woodedge, which dates to 1900, was the elegant residence of William Stone Post (1866–1940), the second child of George and Alice Post. The drawings for this house were signed off on by the firm, but it was almost certainly designed not by the senior Post but by William. Although the house was recognizable as a product of the Post firm's residential work—the columns, the hipped roof with its balustrade, classical proportions, the sense of dignity and purpose—it was also different in some important ways and reflected the individual character of its owner and probable designer, William.

Trained at Columbia University in architecture, William spent a year abroad in preparation for his career. He studied well and developed a talent that was subtle and farsighted, enabling him to produce original work while still adhering to the established principles of his father. William was the first of Post's sons to enter the family firm, in 1891. In 1904 he became a full partner, along with his younger brother, James Otis Post, in what was then named George B. Post & Sons, where he worked until his retirement in 1930. In 1894 William married Lilian Hood Adams, a daughter of the Confederate general John Bell Hood. After her father's death, Lilian was adopted by Mr. and Mrs. Thatcher M. Adams, who, for several years in the 1890s, owned the Post-designed residence in Bernardsville now known as *Stronghold*.

William collaborated with his father on the design of the New York Stock Exchange and the Collegiate Gothic-style City College campus in New York City. And, after their father's death in 1913, William and his brother, James Otis, completed the Wisconsin state capitol project. William also took a leading role in the firm's residential commissions, including many of the more than thirty houses in Bernardsville with which the firm was involved.

At *Woodedge*, the ornate Corinthian columns support an entrance portico that spans the full height of the building, rather than stopping short as they do on many of the Post firm's residential structures. Moreover, the columns and matching pilasters are engaged across the façade of the central block of the house. This design element, along with the shorter, simpler Tuscan-style pilasters on either side of the main block, serves to unify an otherwise wide building and renders it a single whole.

Less obvious, but more significant, are the differences in planning and organization. Most Post houses rely on a central core to provide access to public rooms. *Woodedge*, however, eschews anything other than a narrow transversal service corridor and creates, instead, a lateral sequence of rooms that open directly into one another. This device, somewhat novel even now, imparts a decidedly relaxed aura to the interior, in deliberate contrast to the formality of the exterior, but it also accommodates the single-room depth of the structure, yet another innovative gesture in a building that feels far larger than it is.

This strength, even daring, found in William Post's vision has protected *Woodedge* from many of the modernizations that have damaged other historic structures. Held in the family for more than ninety years, first by William and then his daughter, Eleonora, almost nothing save maintenance was permitted. The owners of the estate during the 1990s were experts in the architecture and decoration of the late-nineteenth century. Aware of *Woodedge's* architectural significance and the rare quality of its many original features and finishes, they saw themselves as curators, not just owners, and did nothing to alter the unique character of the house. It was only in 1998 that a modern kitchen and air-conditioning were installed.

In a 1911 article in Architecture *magazine that com-*
pared the Bernardsville houses of George B. Post
(Claremont), George B. Post Jr. (Kenilwood), *and*
William Stone Post (Woodedge)—*all of which were*
constructed within a four-year period—the editors
remarked: "It is curious to find three houses of so high a
quality of design and of such marked points of difference,
worked out in the same office for people of the same
family, and yet probably each seems to its owner the
most perfect exponent of modern American life."

White Lodge, *the residence of Allison Wright Post, is believed to have been converted from an existing structure on Post's father's property. Wright Post and his family occupied the house from about 1900 to the late 1940s. It burned to the ground in the early 1950s.*

WHITE LODGE

WHITE LODGE was the Bernardsville home of Allison Wright Post (1867–1944), the third of George and Alice Post's five children. Like his stockbroker brother, George Jr., Allison Wright chose a different profession than his father and two other brothers, William Stone and James Otis, who were partners in the architectural firm George B. Post & Sons. But A. Wright Post's name lives on in the Bernardsville area as the author of the memoir, *Recollections of Bernardsville, New Jersey, 1871–1941,* an invaluable record of the settlement and early days of the mountain colony.

A. Wright Post was just four years old when his parents began to summer in Bernardsville in 1871. *Recollections* is full of colorful vignettes of life on the mountain. Post recounts, for instance, the great mid-March blizzard of 1888 when he and his father were snowbound for five days in the family's home, subsisting on the chickens, eggs, and milk that their farmer brought in on a sled. There are also anecdotes of many of the area's prominent early residents—Richard Lindabury, Calvin McMurtry, John Dryden, Frederic Olcott, Coleman Drayton, Grant Schley.

A. Wright Post was born on Long Island, where his family summered before moving to Bernardsville for his mother's health. He graduated from Columbia in 1890 before going on to New York University Law School. After practicing law for several years with the firm of North, Wood & Wagstaff, Post embarked on a career in real estate, establishing a partnership with William Willis Reese. Their firm, Post & Reese, was active in real estate on Manhattan's Upper East Side and in the Somerset Hills.

Post married Katharine Beekman Hoppin, a descendant of the Dutch Beekman family that emigrated to New Amsterdam in the mid-1600s and went on to acquire vast real estate holdings in Manhattan and the Hudson River Valley. Beekman Street in lower Manhattan is named after the family.

As would be expected, *White Lodge* was designed by the Post family's architectural firm. The first reference to the stone-and-stucco residence in the firm's records concerns alterations that were carried out in 1900, about a year after A. Wright and Katharine were married. Additional, and apparently more significant, changes were carried out in 1906. These references, together with a real estate brochure published just a few years after A. Wright Post's death that refers to the house having been rebuilt, suggests that *White Lodge* was built from an existing structure, perhaps a barn or other farm building on the George Post estate. But the finished house, with its massing, classic proportions, strong details, and columned central portico, bore all the hallmarks of a typical Post-designed residence. *White Lodge*, along with the adjacent properties of A. Wright Post's brother, William, and his niece and nephew-in-law, Lilian and Catesby ap L. Jones, formed a family compound on land that had been part of George B. Post Sr.'s estate, *Claremont*, and which commanded some of the best mountaintop views.

A. Wright Post was a keen sportsman and enjoyed all manner of outside activities, but his real passion was lawn tennis. He was captain of the tennis team at Columbia and rose to an amateur ranking of ninth in the world. At *White Lodge*, Post built a grass tennis court, which was frequently in use by the family and visitors. He was actively involved in setting up the area's first country club, the Somerset Hills Country Club, which in its early days on the hill above Ravine Lake included several grass tennis courts and a nine-hole golf course. Post's other consuming interest was gardening. He took great pleasure in *White Lodge*'s large vegetable garden and in the prizewinning fruit cultivated from the apple, peach, and pear orchards that covered many acres of the property.

Post died in 1944. A few years after the war, his widow, Katharine, and their two daughters, Katharine and Muriel, sold the estate. In the early 1950s, the house burned to the ground.

KENILWOOD

ALTHOUGH *Kenilwood* was built by and for the George B. Post family, who owned it for more than eighty years, few estates on the Bernardsville mountain have had such varied, even exotic, owners. Newspaper reports and records of the Post architectural firm indicate that *Kenilwood* was designed in 1901 or 1902 by William Stone Post for his older brother, George B. Post Jr. (1864–1937), and George's wife, Julia Cotton Smith, on land purchased from their neighbor, Percy Rivington Pyne, who built *Upton Pyne*.

Kenilwood was unique among the many residences in the area designed by the Post architectural firm because of its imposing Gothic Revival style. It was a style that William and his father had used several years before in their winning submission for the competition to design the new campus of the City College of New York on St. Nicholas Heights on the Upper West Side of Manhattan. Due to delays in the City College project, however, *Kenilwood* was actually

completed a year or so before work began on the college campus. Tragically, on New Year's Eve, 1902, *Kenilwood,* only just completed, was destroyed by fire. It was thoroughly rebuilt within the original stone walls the following year. Further additions and alterations, designed by the Post firm, were carried out in 1906 and again about five years later. The Posts retained Charles Wellford Leavitt Jr., a self-described "landscape engineer," to landscape the estate. Noted for the diversity of his work and attention to detail, Leavitt designed a formal tree-shaded gravel drive from the road and, on the opposite side of the house, laid out extensive terraced gardens, separated by stone walls, steps, and hedges, that included topiary and rose gardens and a lily pond.

George Post Jr. was a founder, in 1888, along with W. Allston Flagg, a brother of noted architect Ernest Flagg, of the Wall Street brokerage firm Post & Flagg. *Kenilwood* provided a private country retreat for a man much involved in business and public affairs. As family patriarch, after his father's death in 1913, the younger George supported a variety of domestic activities and interests. He retained his seat on the New York Stock Exchange until shortly before his death, but still managed to involve himself in Bernardsville life. He was one of the original organizers, and for a period the president, of the Somerset Hills Country Club, an esteemed trustee in his local parish, St. Bernard's, and the respected breeder and trainer of a beloved pack of beagles.

Post lived at *Kenilwood* until his death, after which his son, George B. Post (1890–1952), occupied the house for fifteen years until his own death. The next owner was the builder's daughter, Harriet Appleton Post (1894–1969). Harriet and her third husband, Sumner Welles, who served as undersecretary of state during the presidency of Franklin D. Roosevelt, carried out extensive redecorations with the assistance of Albert Hadley and his partner, Sis-

ter Parish, née Dorothy Kinnicutt, Mrs. Welles's cousin.

The next inhabitants of the estate were Harriet Welles's son from her first marriage, R. Thornton Wilson Jr. (1923–1996), and his first wife, the legendary Carmel Snow, editor of *Harper's Bazaar.* A generation of America's social and cultural elite came to know *Kenilwood* through the lavish hospitality that was offered there during the Wilsons' ownership. In the early 1980s the firm of Parish-Hadley was retained once again to refurbish the house. Historic pieces were painstakingly restored, and the attic, a virtual museum, was trawled for its many antique treasures collected over the years by a succession of family occupants, many of whom had married into other prominent families along the way.

In the mid-1980s Thornton Wilson reluctantly sold the sixty-five-acre estate to a developer who subdivided the property. The house was modernized and once again redecorated, in a style that critics say compromised Parish-Hadley's elegant work.

The subsequent owner was the reigning world heavyweight boxing champion, Mike Tyson, and his new wife, the actress Robin Givens. The couple embarked on a $1 million facelift of the estate, which was to include the application of 50,000 sheets of gold leaf to the interior fretwork. Only the dining room was completed. For a brief period, *Kenilwood* was catapulted into yet another phase of life as a gathering place for sports and entertainment figures. Martina Navratilova was among the superstars to play tennis on the newly installed court. This exposure reached its culmination when the nation was let inside the house through the televised interview Barbara Walters held with the beleaguered couple. Not long thereafter, their marriage ended, and *Kenilwood* was put on the market once again. At nearly 100 years of age, *Kenilwood* returned to the private world of its origins.

APPLETREES

APPLETREES has two connections that bind it closely to early mountain colony society. Not only is it the work of the architectural firm of George B. Post, but for almost 100 years, *Appletrees* was the home of members of the Turnbull family, early denizens of the area who helped shape the community. The residence was built in 1893 for Ramsay Turnbull (1863–1924) and his wife, Martha Benedict, whose sister Helen married the prominent architect Thomas Hastings. The original architect is not known, although it is believed to have been George B. Post, who designed additions and alterations to the house in 1900–01.

Ramsay and Martha's 1891 wedding was a glittering society event in New York City, attended by former President and Mrs. Grover Cleveland; the famous actor Edwin Booth, brother of John Wilkes Booth; William K. Vanderbilt; the George B. Posts, and the doyenne of New York society at that time, Caroline Schermerhorn Astor. Ramsay's younger brother, Arthur, later married into the Post family and lived over the mountain in Far Hills at *Teviot Farm*.

Ramsay Turnbull graduated from Columbia College in 1884 and worked as a stockbroker in New York City. He was civic-minded and contributed much to the Bernardsville community, one of his greatest contributions being his efforts to improve local roads at a time when there were inadequate township funds to do the job. He was a founder, in 1908, and for years the chair, of the Road and Improvement Society of Mine Mount, the organization that financed the repair and maintenance of roads on the mountain using donations from local residents. Turnbull was also involved in the almost twenty-year campaign to establish a Bernardsville borough—as distinct from Bernards Township—which came to fruition in 1924.

Ramsay Turnbull died long before his wife, who remained in the house until her death, in 1957, at the age of ninety-four. The property then passed on to their daughter, Helen, and her husband, Philip P. Gardiner. Helen Gardiner, who was born in 1893 at *Appletrees*, died there in 1990 at the age of ninety-seven. It was only then that the house was sold out of the family that had built it almost a century before.

Constructed in 1893 and altered
and enlarged seven years later,
Appletrees was occupied by the
family of Ramsay and Martha
Turnbull for close to 100 years.
This image is of the original house
before the two-story pedimented
portico and side wings were added.

The estate's imposing stone water
tower adds a dramatic architectural
touch to the gardens.

The wing and porch on the right in this image of the
rear façade of Appletrees were likely added in 1900—01.

STRONGHOLD

Located on one of the highest points in Bernardsville, the house now called *Stronghold* was built in 1886 for James Coleman Drayton (1852–1934), a New York banker and a son-in-law of William Backhouse Astor and his wife, Caroline Schermerhorn. The Draytons' house, which they named *Crow's Foot*, was designed by George B. Post. It was a two-story, villa-like stone structure with a high tower offering commanding views of the surrounding countryside.

In his memoirs, Post's son, Allison Wright Post, wrote of Drayton: "I never knew a finer gentleman and sportsman." Drayton was fond of shooting and had many hunting dogs, principally setters and Irish terriers, and in 1890 he and George B. Post started the Somerset Kennels on land donated by Post. Although he was "inclined to bookishness" and the quiet pursuits of country life, Drayton became a very public figure because of his marriage to Charlotte Augusta Astor, a union that was destined to be perhaps the most spectacular and newsworthy within the distinguished Astor clan.

In the early 1890s a well-publicized scandal erupted in the Drayton household when Charlotte and a Bernardsville neighbor, Hallett Alsop Borrowe, embarked on a *liaison dangereuse*. Because Charlotte was not only an Astor but a mother of four, and Borrowe was a descendant of an old and respected New York family, the affair was fodder for society's wagging tongues, newspaper front pages, and even, allegedly, servants intent on blackmail.

The two were said to have indiscreetly rendezvoused in New York hotels, while Borrowe, who lived only a "squirrel's scamper" from the Draytons in Bernardsville, frequently paid visits to *Crow's Foot*—lunching there and accompanying Charlotte on carriage drives—when Coleman was out of town. When William Astor learned of the affair, he packed his daughter and Drayton off to London and threatened to cut his daughter out of his will if she did not stop the affair with Borrowe.

Borrowe followed the Draytons to London, meeting there clandestinely with Charlotte. On discovering this, Coleman Drayton challenged Borrowe to a duel in France, where the practice was legal. Despite numerous meetings among their seconds, the Drayton-Borrowe *réparation par les armes* never took place. William Astor suffered a fatal

The semicircular columned portico, designed by George B. Post,
was added to the house for John F. Dryden circa 1899.
Claremont, Post's own house located nearby, featured a similar
curved portico. The irregular rough-faced fieldstone used to
construct Stonghold is said to have been quarried at the site.

heart attack in Paris as the drama was playing out, helping to put a final end to the affair, although he did carry through on his threat to cut his daughter's inheritance, which was later reinstated by her brother.

Charlotte and Coleman sued each other for divorce, which she was granted, although Drayton was awarded the children and substantial funds. She moved to England, where she lived out her life, married to a member of the Haig whiskey family. Borrowe, whose father had grown weary of his son's reckless ways, was sent to work in a menial street-railway job in Newark, where he proved his mettle and went on to marry the daughter of a railroad executive. In 1898 Borrowe joined Theodore Roosevelt's Rough Riders in Cuba, where he distinguished himself. Later, in World War I, he rose to the rank of captain and was awarded the Croix de Guerre.

In October 1892, only seven months after the Drayton-Borrowe affair was splashed across the newspapers, Drayton sold his New Jersey estate, furnishings and all, to a prominent New York lawyer, Thatcher M. Adams, and his wife, Frances Charlotte. Their adopted daughter, Lilian Hood, a daughter of Confederate general John Bell Hood, married George B. Post's son, William Stone Post. The Adamses owned the property for seven years before selling it to the Dryden family, who were to own it for the next forty years.

John Fairfield Dryden (1839–1911) was one of the founders and the third president of the Prudential Insurance Company, serving in that office for thirty years, from 1881 until his death. He also served as a United States senator from New Jersey from 1902 to 1907. Shortly after purchasing the property, Dryden retained George B. Post to design exterior and interior additions and alterations to the house, which Dryden renamed *Stronghold*. Among the distinctive exterior additions were a semicircular columned porch and terraces. The same year, Post designed a new Romanesque-style headquarters building in Newark for Prudential. In 1904, and again in 1916, the Post firm made additional alterations to *Stronghold*.

John Dryden was born in 1839 in Maine of sturdy New England stock. He was educated at Yale, but in his final year was forced to abandon his studies due to ill health. Studying the so-called "prudential" system in England, he became convinced that life insurance could be made available—and affordable—to wage-earners by issuing small policies with weekly premiums. Dryden's plan was taken up by a group of influential businessmen in Newark, New Jersey, and in 1873 the first policy of the Prudential Friendly Society—later to become the Prudential Insurance Company—was written. Known as the "father of industrial insurance" in America, Dryden became the president of Prudential in 1881. During its first twenty-five years of operation, the company's receipts grew from $15,000 to $17 million.

Dryden was active in public affairs throughout his life, and in 1902 he was elected to the United States Senate by the New Jersey legislature to fill the seat of a deceased senator. In the midst of a hard-fought campaign for reelection in 1907, Dryden withdrew because of a deadlock in the state legislature. While serving in the Senate, Dryden, who was a friend of President Theodore Roosevelt, led efforts for passage of the bill creating the Panama Canal, one of Roosevelt's most important projects.

Dryden was married to Cynthia Fairchild, who bore him two children, Cynthia and Forrest, both of whom lived in Bernardsville for much of their lives. John Dryden died in 1911, after which his wife initially moved to New York City while Forrest occupied the Bernardsville property. Dryden's widow eventually returned to *Stronghold* where she remained until her death in 1916. The property passed to Forrest, who was then the president of Prudential, a post he held until retiring in 1922. Forrest died in 1932, after which his wife, Grace, remained in the house until her own death in 1937. The property then passed on to their son, John F. Dryden II.

In 1940, after several years of vacancy and burdened by the costs of upkeep, John F. Dryden II sold *Stronghold* to

*Drawing by the George B. Post
firm of the main entrance
vestibule, which featured grilled
doors and an ornate ceiling.*

*Opposite, above: Gallery looking
toward main staircase. Photo taken
in 1943, shortly after Stronghold
was acquired by Miss Gill's School.*

*Opposite, below: Gallery looking
toward living room, 1943.*

were transported up the mountain from Far Hills and stored in the icehouse under thick coatings of sawdust to prevent melting. Generators, run by gasoline-powered engines, produced electricity. Water from a stream was pumped up to the estate and stored in a water tower, then gravity-fed to the house and other buildings. There was a ten-car garage and a machine shop to repair the cars and farm machinery. Among the many farm and tenant buildings on the estate, there was a horse barn for Dryden's beloved carriage horses and a carriage house. Behind the house was a long carriage road that wound through the woods, along which the Drydens and their guests would often take leisurely drives.

Stronghold was characteristic of George B. Post's work. It was simply planned and strongly detailed. The exterior walls, made of stone said to have been quarried near the site, were irregular and rough-faced fieldstone, which contrasted with the formal stone balustrade of the roof and the refinement of the Corinthian columns. This contrast of practical and classical was abrupt, creating a compelling tension. The elegance of the details, particularly on the interior, contrasted with the bluntness of the plan and the massing, creating a house of great visual interest. The colonnade across the principal façade was delicate, embraced by the massive porte cochère and its paired stone wing. The shallow, sloped roof disappeared behind the cornice balustrade, further emphasizing the direct and forceful character of the house.

The interior of *Stronghold* was distinctive for both its architectural embellishments and its furnishings. Pattern and ornament were present everywhere, from the grilled vestibule door to the plastered and frescoed ceilings. The millwork was ornately carved and minutely detailed. Columns served to help demarcate rooms, as well as provide surface texture where they engaged the wall. The house's tapestries, stained-glass windows, and Persian and Turkish rugs added more color and visual texture. A leaded, stained-glass lay light in the stair hall brought filtered, natural light into the interior of the house.

Miss Gill's School, a private girls' school that had been renting the John F. Talmage estate in Mendham. The thirty-nine-acre property sold for $200,000. The deed of transfer specified that it only be used by the school or as a private residence. Two other dwellings on the *Stronghold* estate, *Boudinot Cottage* and *Fairfield*, were sold separately. *Stronghold* returned to private ownership in 1995, when the school, renamed Gill-St. Bernard's, sold it.

Typical of many of the country houses of the period, under the ownership of the Drydens, *Stronghold* was a working enterprise that was in many respects self-sufficient, with a staff of fifty to keep things running smoothly. There were chickens, pigs, sheep, and cows. A greenhouse, tended by three gardeners, supplied the family homes with cut flowers, and gardens and orchards supplied vegetables and fruits. Ice was harvested several times a year from Ravine Lake and cut into large blocks, which

BOUDINOT COTTAGE

A 1903 ARTICLE IN *Town & Country* magazine featured Bernardsville's flourishing community of wealthy summer residents and their "cottages." Of the house long referred to as the *Boudinot Cottage*, which later became part of the vast *Stronghold* estate, it rhapsodized: "It is vine covered and picturesque and one of the prettiest landmarks in New Jersey." Reminiscent of an English country cottage, the fieldstone house was, until just before the article was written, the home of Miss Jane Johnston Boudinot (c. 1833–1914), a descendent of a key figure in the War of Independence, Elias Boudinot (1740–1821).

Elias's great-grandfather, Elie Boudinot, was a Huguenot who emigrated from France to America in 1687 to escape religious persecution. Elias served in the Continental Congress from 1777–78 and again from 1781–84. During the Revolutionary War, Elias moved his family from Elizabeth to Basking Ridge, New Jersey, where their house, on North Maple Avenue, is still standing. With General George Washington's Morristown headquarters only eight miles away, Martha Washington was said to have been a frequent visitor to the Boudinot house during the Revolutionary War.

In 1782 Boudinot was elected president of the Continental Congress; and the following year signed the Treaty of Paris that formally ended the Revolution and recog-

nized the United States of America. With that act, Boudinot automatically became the first President of the United States in Congress Assembled (George Washington was the first president under the Constitution). After the war, Boudinot served as secretary for foreign affairs and was elected to the country's first Congress under the Constitution. In 1796 President Washington appointed Boudinot director of the United States Mint.

Boudinot's philanthropic work, as much as his contribution to the War of Independence, has ensured him a place in history. He was one of the founders, in 1816, and first president of the American Bible Society. He actively supported the cause of repressed minority groups, including American Indians and exiled Jews. In his will, Boudinot bequeathed much of his estate, which was substantial, to various charities. And, although various days of thanksgiving had been celebrated in various parts of the American colonies long before the Revolution, Boudinot is credited by many with establishing the tradition of a national holiday of thanksgiving. As a congressman, he called on President Washington to proclaim the young nation's first formal observance of "a day of public thanksgiving and prayer, to be observed by acknowledging with grateful hearts the many signal favors of Almighty God, especially by affording them an opportunity to establish a Constitution of Government for their safety and happiness."

Jane Boudinot, the granddaughter of Elias's younger brother, Elisha, was born and raised in Burlington, New Jersey. In 1885 Jane bought the Bernardsville stone cottage and the surrounding fifteen-acre tract from Abraham and Susan McCollum, members of an early settler family. The cottage is thought to date to the late-eighteenth or early-nineteenth century. Jane lived there until 1902 when she sold the property to Col. Anthony R. Kuser, who had recently moved to Bernardsville with his wife, Cynthia Dryden Kuser.

Jane Boudinot was independent minded and lived a life not typical of women of her era. She was vice president of the Colonial Dames of America and wrote several historical works, including a biography of her great-uncle,

The Life of Elias Boudinot, and a memoir of her aunt, Susan Boudinot, who married Washington's attorney general, William Bradford. Through her family's connections, Jane inherited a Charles Wilson Peale portrait of George Washington, which she bequeathed to the Mount Vernon Ladies Association.

Col. Kuser did not own the property for long but transferred it to the estate of his father-in-law, John Dryden. As part of *Stronghold*, the cottage served as a gatehouse at the most westerly entrance to the estate, marked by massive stone pillars similar to those at the other entrances. Later, the name of the cottage was changed to *Honeyfield*, which was engraved into the pillars. The cottage was sold by the Dryden family in the late 1930s.

Fairfield *was added to and altered several times over the years, although the original house is said to have been constructed in the early 1800s. The house was part of the* Stronghold *estate and was owned by the Dryden family for fifty years.*

FAIRFIELD

PART OF THE *Stronghold* estate, *Fairfield* was built in the Colonial Revival style. The original sections of the house date to the early 1800s, but it was added to and altered over the years. In 1905 the firm of George B. Post & Sons designed additions. In 1937 the house was extensively remodeled for John F. Dryden II (1894–1947), the son of Forrest Dryden and grandson of John F. Dryden, under the direction of Josiah R. Brierly, who lived in Bernardsville from 1919 until his death in 1967. Brierly was a partner in the Newark architectural firm of J.H. & W.C. Ely, which designed many commercial buildings as well as the original section of the present Morristown Memorial Hospital; the city halls of Newark and East Orange, New Jersey, and the New Jersey Historical Society building in Newark.

Fairfield, which is a Dryden family name, sits on a slope and is characterized by its generous porches, which almost encircle it. The front porch and portico are classically detailed with fluted Greek Doric columns; a strong, simple entablature, and a Chippendale roof railing. The porches mediate between the house's comfortable and generous interior and the parklike grounds. John Rowlett Brinley, a noted landscape architect who lived in Morristown, planned the gardens and grounds. Brinley's New York firm, Brinley & Holbrook, was involved in the landscape design of many estates in Morris and Somerset counties, including *Stronghold*, *Blythewood*, *Faircourt*, and *Brushwood*.

John F. Dryden II spent much of his career in the insurance business, like his father and grandfather before him. He headed the Industrial Insurance Branch of the Prudential Insurance Company's Washington, D.C., office from 1919 to 1927. He then became president and director of Investors of Washington, an investment firm, although he continued to consult for the insurance industry. Dryden died in Bernardsville after a long illness. In 1948 *Fairfield* was sold by Dryden's widow, Leila, and her second husband, Herbert Wilgus Ballantine, a descendant of the Newark brewing family of the same name

A very comfortable example of Colonial Revival architecture, Fairfield is characterized by its porches, which nearly encircle the house.

FAIRCOURT

EVERY HOUSE has a story to tell. Three mansions atop the Bernardsville mountain—*Faircourt*, *Blythewood*, and *Denbrooke*—tell, among them, at least some of the story of the Kuser family—a true rags-to-riches American immigrant's tale.

In 1848 Rosalia Prieth arrived, penniless, in the United States from the Austrian Tyrol. She met and married Rudolph Kuser, a German mechanical engineer. Anthony Rudolph Kuser and his twin brother, John, were born to Rudolph and Rosalia in 1862 in Newark. A few years later, the family moved, first to Hackettstown then to a farm outside Trenton. Anthony attended public school in Trenton, later working as a "pants presser" and a streetcar conductor.

Anthony R. Kuser's early foray into business was in the brewing industry, working as an agent for a New York brewer and then as a wholesale dealer in the industry. Success in this led to other business ventures, and over the next twenty years, Kuser was involved with many Trenton businesses. Kuser was one of the twenty-four original directors of the Public Service Corporation when it was organized in 1903 and was its vice president for many years. He was an organizer and president of the South Jersey Gas, Electric & Traction Company and a director of the Prudential Insurance Company and the Fidelity Trust Company. The Fox Film Company, which later merged with Twentieth Century, was started with a $200,000 loan from Kuser. Widely known as Colonel Kuser, he acquired his honorary title because he served on the staffs of three New Jersey governors, who appointed him to various state commissions.

Living in Newark during Kuser's rapid climb up the ladder of success was the Dryden family. John F. Dryden was one of the founders of the Prudential Insurance Company and later served as a United States senator from New Jersey. Although Anthony Kuser would have mixed in very different social circles from those of the Drydens, he met and fell in love with their daughter, Susie Fairfield. The couple married in 1896 and initially lived in the Drydens' Broad Street home in Newark.

In 1899 John Dryden purchased a residence on the Bernardsville mountain—the landmark estate that he named *Stronghold*. Three years later, his daughter and son-in-law began acquiring their own property nearby, including the George B. Post family's original Bernardsville home, known as *Claremont Farms*, the old Ballentine farmhouse that had been enlarged and remodeled by the Posts. Records suggest that the Kusers, rather than build an entirely new home, opted to significantly remodel *Claremont*, including a refacing of the dark Victorian exterior with a light-colored neoclassical façade replete with Corinthian-columned porticos. The Kusers renamed the property *Faircourt*, in apparent recognition of the Dryden family name, Fairfield, and Susie's mother's maiden name, Fairchild.

The Kusers carried out extensive landscape work, designed by the New York landscape architecture firm of Brinley & Holbrook. The firm's senior partner, John Rowlett Brinley, who first trained as a civil engineer, was a long-time resident of Morristown who had worked on many engineering projects on large estates in that area before forming his landscape architecture practice with John Holbrook.

Anthony Kuser's abiding love was animals, in particular birds. He contributed much to wildlife protection and preservation and was a longtime member of the Audubon Society and an executive committee member of the New York Zoological Society. According to his one-time daughter-in-law, Brooke Russell Astor, the social highlight of Kuser's year was the summer garden party for zoo members, at which he took delight in talking shop with the ornithologists.

Kuser maintained a private animal park at *Faircourt*, which was open to the public on Sunday afternoons. He had a large private collection of birds, which were housed in aviaries on the estate. Numbering up to 700, the birds represented about 180 varieties and included a world-renowned collection of pheasants—200 birds of forty species. Kuser experimented with breeding, raising, and freeing birds in an effort to reintroduce to New Jersey native birds that had become rare. Kuser also financed a 52,000-mile expedition, begun in 1909, by the ornithologist Charles William Beebe that traveled to twenty Asian countries to study and collect specimens of pheasants.

Sunken garden designed by Brinley & Holbrook.

Aviary, part of the Kusers' private animal park at Faircourt.

The expedition resulted in a beautifully illustrated four-volume work, *A Monograph of the Pheasants*, that was underwritten by Kuser and published by the New York Zoological Society, and which is still considered one of the most authoritative resources on that bird.

Around 1911 Anthony Kuser acquired about 2,000 acres in the Kittatinny Mountains in Sussex County, New Jersey, including High Point, at 1,803 feet the highest point in the state. At about the same time, Kuser's father-in-law, John F. Dryden, acquired an adjoining 7,000-acre tract, intending that the land be a park and game preserve. Dryden died later that year, and the property passed to Kuser, who converted the old High Point Inn into a summer residence and improved the natural landscape with the addition of carriage roads, trails, ornamental trees, and rustic seats. In 1922 the Kusers donated the property—which had by then grown to encompass 10,500 acres—to New Jersey as its first state park, stipulating that all wildlife within it be protected. Not long before his death, Kuser commissioned a 220-foot-high tower, patterned on the Bunker Hill monument at Charlestown, Massachusetts, to be erected at High Point in memory of the soldiers and sailors of New Jersey who lost their lives in combat. The Kuser home, the old High Point Inn, fell into such disrepair that it had to be demolished in the mid-1990s.

In 1916 Susie and Anthony Kuser purchased the Henry Kunhardt estate, *Blythewood*, located just a short distance from *Faircourt*. Three years later, they sold the original *Faircourt* to Ferdinand J. Kuhn and his wife, Lorol Dean. Kuhn had emigrated from Germany in about 1890 and worked in the wool business, managing the Botany Worsted Mills in Passaic, New Jersey. The Kuhns renamed the property *Langstone*, which is inscribed on the brick pillars that once graced the entrance drives and are today among the few remaining vestiges of the original estate.

Lorol Kuhn was an enthusiastic horsewoman, and at her instigation, the stables were meticulously renovated, including, reportedly, the laying of special bricks on the floor for the comfort of the horses. In 1933, not long after the death of Lorol, Ferdinand Kuhn died.

Sometime after Kuhn's death, the property was sold at public auction to a developer who tore down the mansion and subdivided the land. In 1952 Martha and William Dodd bought a seven-acre tract that included the former carriage house, which they renovated and lived in. A miniature campground was established on the property and used by the Somerset Hills Girl Scouts as an official training site.

Little remains today of the Kusers' *Faircourt,* except a few converted outbuildings, the brick entrance pillars, and portions of the original iron fence.

Rather than build a new house, the Kusers are believed to have significantly altered the original house of the George B. Post family, including replacing the dark Victorian exterior with a white classical façade and adding columned porches and porticos (compare with photograph on page 12).

Entrance gates at the corner of Claremont Road and Post Lane.

SARAH CONDICT COTTAGE

THE COLONIAL Revival-style house on the Bernardsville mountain that is held up as a classic George B. Post summer residence is generally referred to as the *Sarah Condict Cottage*. Ironically, while documentation of the house appears in the New-York Historical Society's George B. Post Collection, little is known about its namesake, Sarah Frances Condict (1859–1917). Her name does not appear in the various accounts of life in the mountain colony. Indeed, it seems possible that Sarah either never lived in the house to which her name is given or only lived there briefly; the name of Sarah's older sister, Caroline Ellen Condict (1856–1949), not her own, appears on the deed to the property.

The Condict family—variously spelled Cunditt, Conditt, Condit—came to America from England in the seventeenth century, settling in Newark and eventually spreading out to the Oranges and Morristown. A relative, Dr. Lewis Condict, served as a member and speaker of the New Jersey Assembly and, later, as a United States congressman during the early part of the nineteenth century. Caroline and Sarah's father, Stephen Hayes Condict, was in the saddlery business in Newark and was a director of the Mechanics National Bank of Newark and the Newark Gas Company. Stephen and his wife, Sophia King, had eight children.

The property on which the *Sarah Condict Cottage* was built was once part of the Eliza Ballentine farm, which George B. Post purchased in 1871. In 1899 Sarah's sister, Caroline, bought nine acres from Post. Architectural historians believe that Post's son William—who joined his father's firm in 1891 and is credited with many of the firm's Bernardsville residential commissions—drew up the plans for the cottage. Exterior walls of local fieldstone and stucco, graceful columns and pediments, and a widow's walk that exploits the exceptional views are among its outstanding features. According to the Post firm's archives, the house was completed in 1899. Real estate records show that in 1902, it was leased for $1,800 a year to Dean Sage, a lawyer who was building an estate in nearby Mendham. In 1904, only five years after purchasing the land, Caroline transferred title to Edith Sands Graham, who retained it for the next twenty years.

In 1924 Wyllys Terry and his wife purchased the house. They commissioned the landscape architect Ellen Biddle Shipman to design gardens for the estate. Terry, who was a descendant of the fourth colonial governor of Connecticut, George Terry, was a star athlete at Yale and in 1884 set a record for the longest run in football history—115 yards—achieved by running the length of the field, which was then 110 yards, from five yards behind the goal line. Terry entered the insurance business in New York, eventually heading his own brokerage firm, Terry & Company.

Terry's wife, the former Marie Baldwin, was the daughter of Michigan governor and United States Senator Henry P. Baldwin. Marie's sister, Katherine, married Walter Phelps Bliss, who built the nearby Mendham estate named *Wendover*. Walter Bliss died in 1924, the same year that Wyllys and Marie Terry bought the *Sarah Condict Cottage*. The Terrys, who had three sons—Wyllys Jr., Baldwin, and Walter—sold their Bernardsville house in 1946. It has since changed hands several times. Although extensively modernized, restoration work has been directed at maintaining its architectural integrity.

The Condict home includes several architectural features that were often seen in the residential commissions of George B. Post & Sons, including a two-story columned entrance portico, strong classic details, and a roof railing.

MALVERN

NOT ONLY is the architectural legacy of George B. Post and his sons evident in mansions across the Bernardsville mountain, but Post enticed many friends and relatives to follow his example and establish summer homes in the area. *Malvern* is a good example of this dual influence. The Post firm was commissioned to design the house for Malvina Appleton (1868–1959), a relative by marriage of the Post family.

Miss Appleton, who never married, was the youngest of the four children of Daniel Sidney Appleton and Malvina W. Marshall Appleton. Her paternal grandfather, Daniel Appleton, founded one of the oldest publishing houses in the country, D. Appleton & Company. Records show that in 1898, Miss Appleton, who was from New York City and was much admired by gentlemen, purchased ten acres from George Post. *Malvern* was sited at nearly the highest point on the Bernardsville mountain, with the back of the house facing eastward. On a clear day, it afforded views all the way to New York. Although the mountain is far more forested now than it was 100 years ago, the house still claims these views; the current owners were witness to the burning of the Twin Towers of the World Trade Center on September 11, 2001.

The design of *Malvern* was not as grand as many of the Posts' other residential commissions, but it had a modesty and simplicity befitting a summer cottage for a single lady. Described as Georgian Palladian, the house has many elements characteristic of the Posts—rounded lines, multiple columns, elegant proportions, and beautiful moldings. The original front entrance was a completely circular portico, which was partially eliminated by subsequent owners.

Miss Appleton was an enthusiastic carriage driver, and she had stables and a carriage house built to accommodate this interest. Her prizewinning ponies, named Punch and Judy, rated a mention in A. Wright Post's Bernardsville memoirs: "I well remember . . . Miss Malvina Appleton in her phaeton and canopy with her pair of piebald ponies."

In 1926 *Malvern* was sold to J. Langdon Schroeder, who carried out extensive alterations, adding a wing and reconfiguring many of the rooms. The house was sold in the 1950s and again in 1965.

The original front entrance of Malvern was a complete circular portico. It was later partially eliminated (see page 49).

BOULDERWOOD

T HE IMPOSING Bernardsville mansion known as
Boulderwood was home for more than forty years to
John Augustus Roebling II (1867–1952), grandson of the
designer and son of the builder of the Brooklyn Bridge,
the beautiful suspension bridge that spans the East River
connecting Brooklyn to Manhattan. The bridge—half
again as long as any in existence at the time—was dubbed
"the eighth wonder of the world" when it opened in 1883,
and made the German-American Roebling family famous
around the globe.

The Trenton-based company founded by John A.
Roebling II's grandfather, John Augustus Roebling, pio-
neered the development of "wire rope"—better known

Boulderwood was constructed between 1902 and 1904 for Edward A LeRoy. It was acquired by John A. Roebling II in 1909.

today as cable. In addition to being a boon to suspension-bridge construction, the firm's wire rope also made possible such inventions as the elevator. After John Roebling's death, his son, Col. Washington A. Roebling, took over management of the family business and spent much of the next fifteen years continuing the task his father had started—the design and construction of the Brooklyn Bridge.

John Roebling II became as famous in Bernardsville for his generosity as he was for his family's remarkable feats of engineering. During more than four decades there, Roebling gave magnanimously—and often anonymously—to worthy causes, institutions, and to the poor. Roebling and his first wife, the former Margaret Shippen McIlvaine, moved to *Boulderwood* in 1909. Designed by George B. Post, the mansion had been built between 1902 and 1904 for

Edward A. LeRoy, a businessman. The Roeblings tore down the house's piazza and added a library, office, and laboratory. Years later, a new kitchen wing was constructed.

Roebling worked in his family's business for several years after earning degrees from Rensselaer Polytechnic Institute in civil engineering and chemistry. By the time he arrived in Bernardsville, however, he had left the company to pursue independent scientific research in his own laboratory. Roebling soon developed a reputation in town as a humble, religious man who would rather give than receive. He contributed locally to the fire company, library, police department, churches, Boy Scouts, Morristown Memorial Hospital, and the Red Cross, among other organizations.

Roebling's philanthropy was especially appreciated during the Great Depression of the 1930s. Discreetly, he learned which local families were out of work or needed financial help and saw to it that their bills were paid or that jobs were offered to them. He even bailed out the financially troubled Bernardsville National Bank. Roebling was said to be as generous with his estate as he was with his money. Picnickers would often go to a beautiful area of the property known as the "north fields," and Roebling, who liked to read there on summer afternoons, would himself turn away from, rather than disturb, the trespassers. He was a lover of wildlife and would buy 100-pound sacks of walnuts, which he would feed to squirrels and chipmunks out of his hand.

Long after Roebling's death, *Boulderwood* was subdivided into twenty-six smaller lots. The mansion remains in private ownership on fourteen acres.

The original Kirkpatrick house, dating from 1765, is the gable wing at the right. The central section with two-story columned porch, the left gable wing, and the porte cochère, all designed by George B. Post & Sons, were added in 1900 by the Squibb family.

KIRKPATRICK HOUSE / WELWOOD

FEW PRE-REVOLUTIONARY HOUSES can be accurately dated, but when David Kirkpatrick (1723–1814) and his wife, Mary, built their fieldstone homestead, they had their initials and that year's date inscribed in the stone lintel above the doorway: "DMK 1765." It is also fortunate for local historians that, more than 100 years later, a Kirkpatrick descendent, Jacob, documented the arrival and settlement of his Scottish ancestors in this country. Thanks to his efforts, much is known about this family that contributed so much to the community, the church, and the judiciary of early America—and whose Bernardsville house is one of the area's oldest homesteads.

In 1736 David Kirkpatrick's father, Alexander, fled religious persecution in Scotland for America. A strict Presbyterian, Alexander had taken part in a failed Jacobite rebellion against the English throne. Alexander, his wife, and their son David sailed from Ireland to New Castle, Delaware, then made their way on foot through Philadelphia to New Jersey through heavily forested terrain with little sign of human habitation, except for the Indian trails they followed. Eventually they came upon a spring near a stream at the foot of a mountain that seemed to provide everything they were looking for. That stream was Mine Brook, and the mountain was the Bernardsville mountain.

The Kirkpatricks initially leased 140 acres from Richard and William Penn, heirs of William Penn, the English Quaker and founder of the colony of Pennsylvania. By the terms of their lease, the Kirkpatricks were required to plant an apple orchard of about forty-five trees—one for every three acres. They built a log house and a combination grist and saw mill—among the first in the area—and lived out their days there, acquiring legal title to the property in 1747.

Alexander died in 1758, leaving his widow and five children. It was the second son, David, who with his Scottish wife, Mary, built the two-story stone homestead that stands today. It had two large chimneys, one at either end, and thick, sturdy walls of sandstone and mortar. The floors were of double-layered white-oak planks. David was a stern, hard-working, churchgoing man who became a member of

the state legislature. He is said to have planted walnut trees out of which he sawed boards for his own coffin. He chose to walk everywhere and often walked to the Presbyterian church in Basking Ridge while his family rode.

It was David's son Andrew (1756–1831) who made his mark on America's evolving judicial system. Andrew was a student at Princeton, then called the College of New Jersey, to which he would walk the thirty miles from home at his father's insistence. After graduating from Princeton, Andrew studied theology, as was his father's wish, but after six months realized this was not his true calling and switched to law. So displeased was David that he expelled his son from the family home. But this did not deter Andrew, who was admitted to the New Jersey bar in 1785 and entered private practice in Morristown. In 1798 Andrew became an associate justice on the New Jersey Supreme Court. Six years later he was elected chief justice, an office he held for the next twenty-one years. Judge Kirkpatrick, known for his conservatism, was a supporter of the whipping post and capital punishment. He was an outstanding practitioner of the law, and his decisions reflected careful research and sharp reasoning.

David Kirkpatrick lived in the family homestead until his death in 1814. In 1852 title to the property was transferred from the Kirkpatrick family to Henry Baird, who enlarged the house. The Welwood family owned the property by the end of the nineteenth century, and in 1897 sold it to Charles F. Squibb, whose family fortune had been made in the chemical industry. Soon after purchasing the house, which he named *Welwood,* after the previous owners, Squibb commissioned the architectural firm of George B. Post & Sons to draw up plans for a substantial addition and alterations. At about the same time, a septic system was added, designed by George Washington Goethals, the Brooklyn-born engineer who oversaw the construction of the Panama Canal. Among the subsequent owners of the property were the Edward Packard family and Chauncey R. McPherson, from Elizabeth, New Jersey.

Though substantially altered and expanded over the years, the stone Kirkpatrick homestead still reflects the strong and sturdy qualities of its original owners.

EDWIN A.S. LEWIS HOUSE

THE RESIDENCE that was home to Judge Edwin Augustus Stevens Lewis (1870–1906) was yet another Bernardsville mountain summer cottage for which the original plans bore the signature of the George B. Post architectural firm. Many of the architectural elements associated with the Posts' residential work are there: the widow's walk, fanlight French doors, waved pediment, and pilasters.

Lewis and his wife, Alice Stuart Walker, were drawn to Bernardsville by family connections. On the side of his mother, Mary Picton Stevens Lewis, a daughter of Col. Edwin A. Stevens and his first wife, Edwin Lewis was a descendent of the famous Stevens family of engineers and inventors from Hoboken. Three of Edwin's uncles and an aunt, all children of Col. Stevens and his second wife, also built mansions on the Bernardsville mountain (see The Stevens Family at page 77).

On the side of his father, Edward Parke Custis Lewis, who was a colonel in the Confederate Army and who later served as minister to Portugal in President Cleveland's administration, Edwin Lewis was a descendant of both George and Martha Washington.

Edwin's sister, Esther Maria Lewis, was married to Charles Merrill Chapin, who around 1895 bought large tracts of land on the mountain and built a summer house. In 1898 Lewis and his wife commissioned Post to design a summer cottage on land that was conveyed to them by the Chapins. The house was located on a hillside to take advantage of mountain views and breezes. The fieldstone used for the twenty-four-inch-thick foundations was transported up the Bernardsville mountain by the wagonload.

Edwin Lewis accomplished much in his short life.

After being graduated from Princeton and New York Law School, he was admitted to the bar in 1894 and was named a counselor in 1897. Lewis, who was a partner in the Hoboken law firm of Lewis, Besson & Stevens, was counsel to the Hoboken Land and Improvement Company, a corporation formed by the Stevens family in 1838 to manage their extensive landholdings and business interests in that city. He also served as counsel to Hoboken's Board of Health and to the Fidelity and Casualty Company of New York. In 1898 Judge Kirkpatrick—a great-grandson of David Kirkpatrick who built the Bernardsville home known as the Kirkpatrick homestead—appointed Lewis referee in bankruptcy for Hudson County, New Jersey. In 1904 Lewis was a delegate to the Democratic National Convention. He was a charter member of the New Jersey State Bar Association and served as president of the Bar Association of Hudson County, a position he held at the time of his death, in 1906, at the age of only thirty-six.

After Lewis's death, his wife remained in the Bernardsville house, raising their two sons. The property stayed in the Lewis family's possession until 1937, when it was sold to Edwin and Ruth Faulkner. Edwin Faulkner, who died in a plane crash along with his daughter, was mayor of Bernardsville from 1955 to 1958.

In January 2001 a blaze started in the basement garage of the house when hot ashes from a fireplace ignited. Despite the efforts of about 100 firefighters, the house burned to the ground. In a sadly ironic twist, it was said to have been the worst house fire in Bernardsville in the forty years since *Dunleith*, the house across the road built by Charles M. Chapin and his wife, Esther Maria Lewis Chapin—Edwin Lewis's sister—was destroyed by fire.

Architect Henry Janeway Hardenbergh designed and built his first summer house in Bernardsville in the 1880s.
After that house burned, in 1906 he built the present structure (above), naming it Renemede.

RENEMEDE

THE RENEMEDE ESTATE in Bernardsville was home to one of the great architects of his time: Henry Janeway Hardenbergh (1847–1918). He was the visionary behind New York's Plaza hotel, the original Waldorf and Astoria hotels (on the site now occupied by the Empire State Building), and the Dakota apartment building, among others. In the Somerset Hills, his work includes the Olcott School and St. Bernard's parish house in Bernardsville. In addition, he collaborated with Guy Lowell in the design of the Ladd mansion in Peapack-Gladstone, known as *Natirar*.

Hardenbergh built *Renemede* in the 1880s and had it rebuilt in 1906 after the original house was destroyed by fire. The main house was a two-and-a-half-story frame-and-stucco building with high-peaked gables adorning its façade. The sixty-eight-acre estate's hilltop setting afforded magnificent views of winding drives, cascading waterfalls, stone bridges, formal gardens with fountains, open lawns, windswept fields, and leafy woodlands. The dwelling was primarily a weekend and summer home for Hardenbergh and his wife, Emily Irene Leeds Keene, serving as a respite from Manhattan where they maintained a year-round residence. There were several cottages at *Renemede* as well as a stone storage barn, laundry

building, stable, garage, chicken coops, and sundry other outbuildings. One of the cottages on the grounds was named *The Villino* by Hardenbergh. It was designed by George B. Post for George B. Salisbury in 1897. Hardenbergh bought the cottage in 1909, and in his will conveyed it and *Renemede* to his brother, William P. Hardenbergh.

At *Renemede*, Hardenbergh's recreational activities included photography—he had a darkroom constructed at the side of the main house—and overseeing the estate's landscaping, in which he had a keen interest. Hardenbergh was closely involved with St. Bernard's Church as a worshiper, trustee, and architect of the parish house. In addition, he gave the church its lectern, bible, and choir stalls and recognized it in his will.

This generous attitude was appreciated by *Renemede*'s workers, who described "Mr. Henry" as a robust, energetic man who was a fair-minded, down-to-earth employer. According to his chauffeur, Alfred Wohlwend of Bernardsville, "he was a real gentleman, and in many ways a friend as well as an employer." Although not a tall man, Hardenbergh had the refined air of an aristocrat, often wearing a dark suit, starched high collar and pearl stickpin, and sporting an immaculately groomed handlebar moustache, in counterpoint to his bald head.

Born in New Brunswick, New Jersey, Hardenbergh was descended from Dutch settlers who came to New York state in the middle of the seventeenth century. He was a great-great-grandson of the Reverend Jacob Rutsen Hardenbergh, a founder and first president of Queens—later Rutgers—College. After attending the Hasbrouck Institute in Jersey City, Hardenbergh entered the New York office of Detlef Lienau, who was educated at the École des Beaux-Arts in Paris under the famous neo-Greek architect Henri Labrouste. Hardenbergh opened his own New York firm in 1871.

With a career that stretched from the post-Civil War years through World War I, Hardenbergh saw vast changes in America's urban landscape. As cities grew and buildings grew taller with the introduction of steel-frame construction, architects were presented with the challenge of designing beautiful and functional multi-storied structures. Hardenbergh was at the forefront of an experimental

movement that applied historical styles in a highly original fashion. His greatest influence was as a designer of luxury hotels and apartment buildings.

The renowned Dakota apartment building in New York, designed by Hardenbergh, was constructed in 1884 and was one of the city's earliest luxury apartment buildings and one of the first to have an elevator. Over the years many celebrity residents, including most famously John Lennon and Yoko Ono, have lived in the French chateau- and German Renaissance-inspired building on Seventy-second Street and Central Park West.

In 1907 the French Renaissance-style Plaza Hotel opened its doors along New York's Fifth Avenue and Central Park South. The landmark hotel's tall gables and projecting wings secured Hardenbergh's place as one of the premier hotel designers of the Edwardian era. The *New York Architect* noted: "It is probably not an exaggeration to say that H. J. Hardenbergh, of New York, is the best-known hotel architect in America." Some of his other

designs were the Copley-Plaza in Boston, the Raleigh and Willard hotels in Washington, D.C., and the 50,000-seat Palmer Memorial Stadium at Princeton University, which was torn down in 1997.

Often described as an interior and exterior decorator rather than an architect, Hardenbergh carefully chose the details of his buildings right down to the design of a fireplace's mantel or the motif of a carved doorknob. He also understood the need for function and created detailed standards for modern hotel designs. In his most famous buildings, he made personal statements by using historical sources, especially European Renaissance styles.

Although he found global fame as an architect, Hardenbergh was also drawn to acting. "He threw up the choice of becoming a great Hamlet and became an architect," said Judge S. D. McConnell at a dinner honoring Hardenbergh. The theater's loss turned out to be the architectural world's gain.

Opposite, above: Rear façade, as originally designed by Henry J. Hardenbergh.

Opposite, below: Rear façade in recent years.

The Villino, *a cottage designed by George B. Post for George B. Salisbury in 1897, later acquired by Henry J. Hardenbergh and incorporated into his* Renemede *estate.*

HILL FARM COTTAGE

ONCE THE HOME of Eliza McCormick Cameron Bradley (1857–1955), the widow of William Hornblower Bradley (1854–1889), the original section of this Bernardsville mountain residence is believed to date to the 1780s.

Both Bradleys were from distinguished families. Eliza's father, J. Donald Cameron, and her grandfather, Simon Cameron, both served as United States senators from Pennsylvania and as secretaries of war, Donald serving under President Ulysses S. Grant and Simon under Abraham Lincoln. William Bradley, an attorney in Newark, was the son of United States Supreme Court Justice Joseph P. Bradley and the grandson of Joseph C. Hornblower, a chief justice of the New Jersey Supreme Court. One of William's forebears, Josiah Hornblower, came to America from England in 1753, bringing with him what was said to have been the first steam engine in this country, which was used to pump out a flooded copper mine near Passaic, New Jersey.

Eliza Bradley's younger sister Margaretta was married to J. William Clark, president of the Clark Thread Company of Newark, and records suggest that Margaretta enticed her widowed sister to Bernardsville, where the Clarks already owned a summer residence. In 1899 the Clarks conveyed forty acres to Eliza Bradley, and the following year William Stone Post, of the architectural firm of George B. Post & Sons, carried out extensive alterations to the existing eighteenth-century house on the property.

In 1923 Eliza Bradley sold the estate to Reginald B. Lanier and his wife, Helen, of New York, who retained ownership until 1955, when the house was sold to William Emlen Roosevelt and his wife, Arlene. Emlen Roosevelt, a distant relative of President Theodore Roosevelt, was an investment banker with Roosevelt & Son, a firm founded in 1797 by his great-great-great-great grandfather, Jacobus.

In 1900 William Stone Post, of the New York architectural firm George B. Post & Sons, made extensive alterations to the original home, which is said to date to the 1780s.

CAMPBELL HOUSE

One of several Bernardsville families that were drawn to the Somerset Hills through an association with the prominent Stevens clan of Hoboken were the Campbells. Born in Louisiana, Palmer Campbell (1856–1925) moved with his parents—William Patrick Campbell and Catherine Elizabeth Smelt Beers—to the United Kingdom as a child, remaining there until his mid-teens, when the family moved to Hoboken. After finishing his schooling, in 1876 Campbell took up employment with the Hoboken Land & Improvement Company, which managed the property and investments of the Stevens family of inventors and engineers. Campbell rose to become president of the company, with which he was associated for fifty years. With his brother Herbert, Palmer also founded Campbell Stores Inc. in Hoboken.

In 1899 Palmer Campbell and his wife, Jean Eno, bought land in Bernardsville for their summer home, acquiring a forty-acre farmstead from her parents, who had acquired it the year before, and a smaller adjoining tract from Robert L. Stevens. The Campbells eventually acquired an estate of more than 200 acres. A large portion of the land had once been part of the farm of the McMurtry family, which acquired it in the 1740s. Robert McMurtry (1749–1822) is credited with building the original part of the Campbells' house in about 1779. The architectural firm of George B. Post & Sons carried out exterior and interior renovations and additions to the house in 1899–1900, shortly after the Campbells acquired the property.

The Campbells had a son, Eno (1895–1984), who served as mayor of Bernardsville from 1945 to 1946. Eno, who was married to Rachel Hall Slack Perrine, bred foxes on the family farm, establishing a company called Somerset Silver Foxes Inc. Eno and Rachel lived in the main residence until 1960 and thereafter across the road in the coachman's house, which they enlarged.

The core of the Campbells' house was constructed circa 1779 for the McMurtry family. The house was enlarged and altered for the Campbells—including the addition of an octagonal porch—by George B. Post in 1899–1900.

STONEHYRST

Water tower.

Stonehyrst, a twenty-room English Tudor house situated on rolling land with views across the Somerset Hills, was designed by Schickel & Ditmars of New York as the country residence of Julius Albert Stursberg (1852–1929). Stursberg made his fortune in sugar refining, but had wide business interests. He served as vice president and director of the South Porto Rico Sugar Company, vice president of the American Enameled Brick and Tile Company, president of the Livingston Worsted Company in Rhode Island, and treasurer and director of the Hermann Stursberg Realty Company.

Although he also maintained a residence in New York City, Stursberg was an active member of the community in Bernardsville, where he summered for nearly thirty-five years until his death in 1929. Wilhelmina Stursberg, one of his three daughters, married the architect Eugene Waterman Mason, who, early in his career, worked for the firm of Carrère & Hastings. In the 1920s, the Masons designed and built their own house on the Stursberg estate.

Built about 1895, *Stonehyrst* is a half-timbered stucco structure above a fieldstone base. Patterned brick chimneys punctuate the slate roof. The combination of materials creates a richly textured façade. Although the massing is simple and the proportions are strong, the house is not heavy in appearance because the exterior walls are broken by cross gables that interrupt the eave and extend into the roof. Smaller dormers align with windows below, and the multiple chimneys are uniformly ordered. The percentage of window openings in the façade is extensive, particularly for a house of its era. In addition to providing ample daylight to the interior, the series of triple-wide double-hung windows, in conjunction with the pattern of the half-timbering, creates a visual lightness for an otherwise massive structure.

William Schickel, like Julius Stursberg a native German, began his architectural career in 1870, at the age of twenty, with Richard Morris Hunt. Hunt, one of the most respected architects of his day, designed *Biltmore* in Asheville, North Carolina, for George Washington Vanderbilt, the United States Military Academy at West Point, and the base of the Statue of Liberty. With Isaac E. Ditmars, a native of Nova Scotia, Schickel established an architectural practice in New York in 1885. Together, the architects completed numerous projects in New York City and New Jersey, including the New York churches of St. Ignatius Loyola, St. Monica, and St. Joseph; residences for Thomas Fortune Ryan, John D. Crimmins, and Isaac Stern; and buildings for St. Vincent's and Lenox Hill hospitals in New York. Their most significant work was the Cathedral of the Sacred Heart in Newark.

Stonehyrst was typical of the period in that it encompassed a large tract of land and multiple buildings. The outbuildings consisted of houses for caretakers and staff, a greenhouse, a stable, and a variety of utility structures. Although not completely self-sufficient, the estate supplied many of its own needs. The water system was extensive, with pipes running from a pump house at the wellhead below the main house to all the principal structures on the property, including six residences. A stone tower, on the highest elevation of the estate, stored the water. It was not until the early 1980s, when the Eugene Mason property passed out of the Stursberg family, that the water system was finally disconnected. The tower still stands, a reminder of both the extent of the engineering required to satisfy an estate's needs and the high quality of the stonemason's work.

Although certainly comfortable in its layout and appointments, *Stonehyrst* was typical of the summer cottages of the mountain colony in that it was not opulent, as were the cottages of Newport. Although now situated on only a fraction of its original 108 acres, the house remains in good condition, an exemplar of the strong and coherent architecture common to the finest of mountain colony estates.

The New York architectural firm of Schickel & Ditmars designed Stonehyrst for the family of Julius Stursberg in 1895.

Haley Fiske's architects at Overcross, Napoleon Le Brun & Sons, also designed St. Bernard's (Episcopal) Church in Bernardsville and the New York headquarters of the Metropolitan Life Insurance Company, of which Fiske was the president.

OVERCROSS

THE SPRAWLING gentleman's estate on the Bernardsville mountain created by Haley Fiske (1852–1929) was a testament to his wealth, his large family, and his love of the countryside. Fiske presided over the Metropolitan Life Insurance Company at a time when it was the largest financial institution in the world. He not only made extensive contributions to public-health education, but is also credited with helping to increase the life expectancy of Americans.

Fiske's ancestors, from Suffolk, England, settled in Salem, Massachusetts, in the seventeenth century. Haley Fiske, who was born in New Brunswick, New Jersey, received his degree from Rutgers College in 1871. He studied law in New York before joining the firm of Arnoux, Ritch & Woodford where he demonstrated unusual ability as a trial lawyer. Fiske was assigned to take charge of litigation for Metropolitan Life, a client of the firm's. Over the years, he developed a broad understanding of the insurance business in general, and Metropolitan Life in particular, and in 1891 was brought in as vice president of the company. Fiske made huge contributions to the insurance industry and helped to develop Metropolitan Life from a relatively small stock institution with capital of $2 million to a mutual company with assets of nearly $4 billion and nearly 43 million policies. At the time of Fiske's death, Metropolitan Life controlled 17 percent of the life-insurance market.

Fiske initiated a health campaign to increase the longevity of Metropolitan Life policyholders, in particular working men and their families, who made up about a quarter of its policyholders. The company distributed millions of health leaflets, dispatched nurses to the industrial centers of the country, and, in a groundbreaking move, used the radio to disseminate health information. Another company initiative during Fiske's tenure as president was the investment of $7.5 million in New York apartment buildings, which were then rented at no more than nine dollars a room. Between 1911 and 1927, the life expectancy of Metropolitan Life's industrial blue-collar policyholders increased by nine years.

Fiske was married twice, first in 1879 to Mary Garratena, who died in 1886. The following year he married Marion Cowles Cushman, the daughter of Archibald Falconer Cushman of New York. The Fiskes made their home in New York City, but beginning in 1892 they bought several large tracts of land in Bernardsville, including what had been the sixty-five-acre farm and homestead of the McWilliams family, two descendants of which were builders who constructed several of the large estates on Bernardsville mountain. An existing Colonial Revival home on the property was expanded and altered by the prominent New York architectural firm of Napoleon Le Brun & Sons, transforming it into a rambling twenty-eight-room country mansion with balconies, balustrades, Ionic columns, and ornate molding, inside and out. In 1916 the Fiskes retained the architectural firm of George B. Post & Sons to design alterations to the house.

The Le Brun firm had also designed the Metropolitan Life Insurance Company's new headquarters on Madison Square in New York in 1892, as well as the adjoining tower, built in 1909, that briefly reigned as the world's tallest building. In Bernardsville, the LeBrun firm designed the Early English Gothic-style St. Bernard's Church in 1897. The selection of LeBrun as the church's architect was no doubt greatly influenced by Haley Fiske, one of the founding trustees of the parish.

Thanks to the existence of a real estate brochure dating to the sale of *Overcross* in the 1930s after Fiske's death, much is known about the elegant summer residence that the Fiskes established for themselves and their six children. The brochure reads: "With easy accessibility over magnificent macadam highways, few private estates in the entire state of New Jersey compare with it in location and splendor of appointment." The brochure went on to note that the estate can be "instantly recognized by the numerous lilac trees that border the main road." The property included a vineyard and orchards of peaches, plums, pears, apricots, and cherries for consumption during the summer and for bottling and preserving to supply the Fiskes' New York household during the winter months.

Overcross was a veritable village of farm buildings and outbuildings. There was a superintendent's cottage at the entrance to the estate, a smoke house and wood house—"both of native stone that lend a picturesque, rural, and romantic atmosphere"—a garage, and a barn to accommo-

date the cows that produced the high-grade milk the farm sold. There was a tool house and a steam-heated coach barn with stalls for farm and saddle horses and staff apartments. There were two dog kennels and runs for the cocker spaniels that Mrs. Fiske bred. Behind the mansion was a laundry house containing a root cellar, a cold-store room, and accommodation for the chauffeur. Nearby were a wood-storage shed, a coal-storage shed, and an icehouse, which stored the ice harvested each winter from the estate's pond.

The gardens combined formal and informal elements. A long flight of steps led down through the terraced garden, which was filled with rose and peony beds, cedar and privet hedges, green English ivy, and masses of forsythia. There was a brook and trout pond surrounded by a "wild garden, filled with evergreens, rhododendrons, violets, and other wood species." In the main gardens were a child's playhouse, a teahouse, a sundial bed, three fountains, four pools, and "a sheltered amphitheatre for outdoor dramatics." There was also a tennis court on which Fiske played several times a week until a few years before his death.

The house itself was "designed in the spirit of the best colonial traditions and of such quiet, dignified character, that immediately indicates it to be the home of a gentleman of refinement," enthused the brochure, which described the architectural style as "formal colonial or Georgian." The wainscoted and paneled dining room was particularly attractive: "A fireplace on one side is an assurance of cheerful comfort; a Dutch door communicates with an open porch overlooking a garden; and windows at one end offer a rare view of the country-side." There was a bowling alley in the basement, a private chapel off the living room, and a walkway on the roof, reminiscent of Atlantic Coast "shore" houses.

Fiske died suddenly from a heart attack outside his Manhattan home. It was fitting that he had just returned from High Mass at St. Mary the Virgin Episcopal Church, of which he was a warden and for fifty-five years the treasurer, and which had been designed some thirty-five years before by his architects of choice, Napoleon LeBrun & Sons. Fiske was a deeply religious man, well read in theology and church history, and a leading layman of the Anglo-Catholic wing of the Protestant Episcopal Church. He was on the first board of trustees of St. Bernard's Episcopal Church in Bernardsville, and several items in the church were given by him or in his memory. The twelve-ton gold-plated bronze doors of the central portal of the Cathedral of St. John the Divine in New York were given in his memory.

A subsequent owner of *Overcross* tore down most of the additions to the main house that had been put on by Fiske, thus returning it to its original size.

Opposite: The Fiskes retained the architectural firm of Napoleon Le Brun & Sons to alter the original house they had acquired in 1892—the central section with three large dormer windows—and to add extensive Colonial Revival wings.

Above: Rear façade with view of the neighboring estate, Stonehyrst, in upper left.

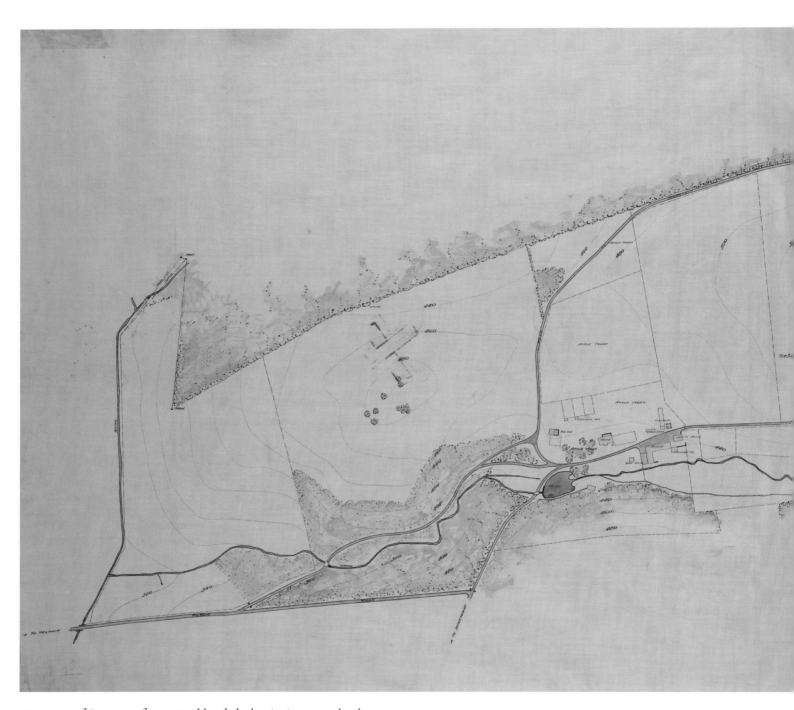

Survey map of Overcross *from 1916. Although the drawing is not reproduced to the original scale, the estate exceeded one mile in width from southeast to north-west. The land and buildings near the pond shown on this page later formed the core of* Little Brook Farm, *the estate of Dr. and Mrs. Frank Lusk Babbott.*

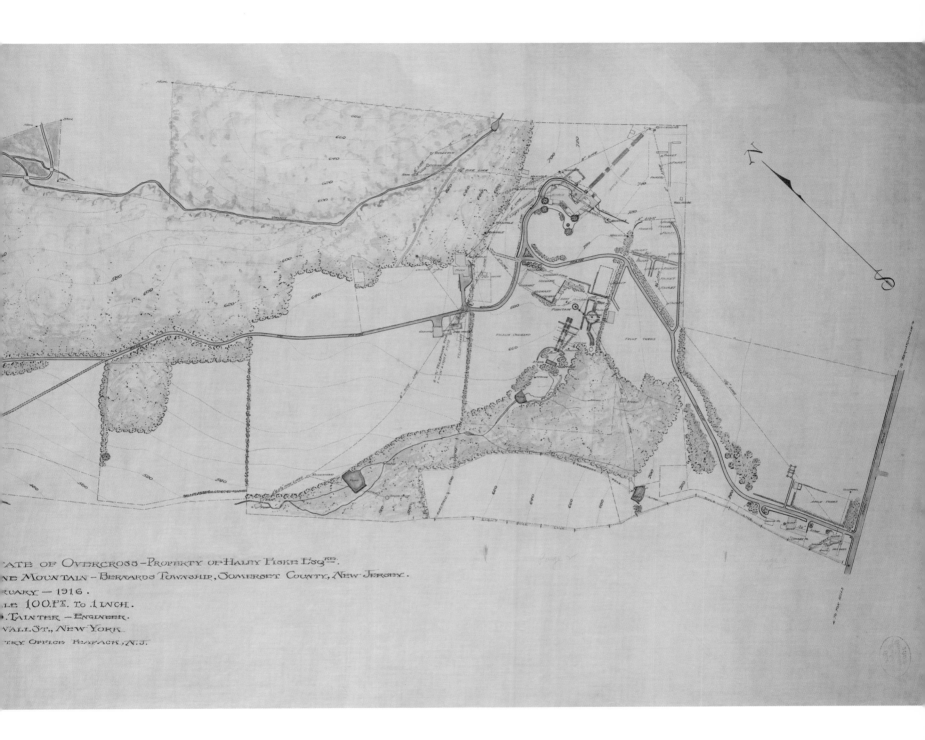

...ATE OF OVERCROSS — PROPERTY OF HALEY FISKE ESQ.

...NE MOUNTAIN — BERNARDS TOWNSHIP, SOMERSET COUNTY, NEW JERSEY.

...RUARY — 1916.

...LE 100 FT. TO 1 INCH.

...TAINTER — ENGINEER.

...VALL ST., NEW YORK.

...TRY OFFICE PEAPACK, N.J.

PEACHCROFT

THE STRIKING fieldstone estate on the Bernardsville mountain known as *Peachcroft* was once owned by John William Clark (1867–1928), president of the Clark Thread Company of Newark. This American branch of the family firm—which originated as Clark Thread Works in Paisley, Scotland—was established in the United States by Clark's father, William. The company has its roots in the late-eighteenth century when Napoleon forbade the exportation of silk to Britain, thereby forcing the company to import Egyptian cotton, which was then spun into thread. By the 1840s the company had family members in America and other countries acting as selling agents, and by the 1860s it began manufacturing thread in the United States.

Born in Newark, J. William Clark started in the family business after completing his education at the university at Bonn, Germany, and served for many years as director and treasurer of the company. Upon the death of his cousin, W. Campbell Clark, who was then president, J. William Clark was chosen to run the company in 1913. For many years the Clark family resided in a Newark mansion on Mount Prospect Avenue built by Clark's father in the early 1880s. After it was sold in 1912, J. William Clark moved his family permanently to *Peachcroft* in Bernardsville. In the 1970s the Newark house was designated a National Historic Landmark and restored for use by the North Ward Educational and Cultural Center.

Peachcroft was built about 1907 on the foundations of the Clarks' previous house, which had burned down. The seventeen-room mansion, styled after an English manor house, presided over more than 300 acres. The structure, built of local fieldstone, was capped by a slate roof, presenting an impressive fireproof façade. The house's entrance, with a painted-brick floor, led into a paneled reception hall paved with red tile. There was a library with beamed ceilings, a living room with a white-marble fireplace, and a bookshelf-lined billiard room. Like many estate houses of its era, *Peachcroft* had a wine cellar, telephone room, servants' sitting room, master bedroom with sun deck,

preserve room, and a dumbwaiter. There was a wing for the servants, a two-family tenant house, and a five-room house for farm laborers. As a working farm, *Peachcroft* had sheep, cows, and chickens.

In 1889 J. William Clark married Margaretta Cameron, a daughter of United States Senator J. Donald Cameron of Pennsylvania, who served as secretary of war under Ulysses Grant. In turn, Donald Cameron's father, Senator Simon Cameron, served as secretary of war under President Lincoln. William and Margaretta Clark had three sons: John Balfour, James Cameron, and William. John and James settled in the Somerset Hills and joined the family business. John was active in the management of the Newark plant of the Clark Company, and James was head of the Spool Cotton Company of New York, a subsidiary of the Clark concern. In 1953 Clark Thread Company and J. & P. Coats, Inc., both of which John B. Clark had served as president, merged to form Coats and Clark Inc.

The Clark's third son, William, was appointed, at age thirty-two, to the New Jersey Court of Errors and Appeals. Two years later he was appointed to the Federal District Court in Newark and later elevated to the United States Court of Appeals for the Third Circuit by President Franklin Roosevelt. Clark served in World War I and as an army colonel in World War II. After the Second World War, he was appointed chief justice of the Allied Appeals Court at Nuremberg, Germany. He married Marjory Blair, daughter of financier C. Ledyard Blair, in 1913. Eight hundred guests were invited to the elegant wedding, and a special train was leased to transport guests from Hoboken to *Blairsden*, the Blairs' Peapack estate. The Clarks settled in Princeton, New Jersey.

The patriarch of the family, J. William Clark, died suddenly of a heart attack in 1928 while at *Peachcroft*. The estate remained in the Clark family until after the death of Margaretta, in 1941. It has since had several owners, including Philip Cortney, president of the cosmetics company, Coty, who sold the estate in 1952.

Peachcroft was built of stone circa 1907 on the foundation of the Clark's previous wood-frame house, which had burned down.

Annandale, *the Robert Livingston Stevens house.*

THE STEVENS FAMILY

MUCH HAS BEEN WRITTEN about the famous Stevens family of inventors, engineers, and public servants that has long been associated with Hoboken, New Jersey, and has been called America's first family of invention. Several members of the Stevens clan established a family compound on the Bernardsville mountain in the late 1800s. Those who were attracted to the thriving summer colony in the Somerset Hills were the grandchildren and great-grandchildren of Col. John Stevens (1749–1838), a visionary engineer and pioneer in the development of steamboat and railroad transportation. The colonel, as he was known because of his service in the Revolutionary War, was the grandchild and namesake of John Stevens who emigrated from England to America in 1699. Although the Stevens family is best known for its inventions and engineering acumen, later generations of the family living in Bernardsville made their marks in the world of politics and diplomacy.

The land that is now Hoboken—the name being an amalgamation of the Dutch and Indian words for what was originally an island separated by marshes on the west and the Hudson River on the east—was conveyed in 1663 by Peter Stuyvesant, governor of Nieuw Amsterdam, to his sister, Anna, whose first husband was Samuel Bayard. In 1784 the 689-acre property—known as the "isle of Hoboc"—then owned by William Bayard, Anna and Samuel's great-great-grandson, was declared forfeit and sold at public auction. William, known as "Weeping Willie" for having lost his prized property, had supported the British in the Revolution and fled the country after the war. The approximately mile-square property was bought by Col. Stevens, who had served in New Jersey's Provincial Congress in 1775 and as New Jersey's trusted "Treasurer on Horseback" during the war. Stevens initially set about developing the property as a riverside resort, building his own home on the promontory above the Hudson that came to be called Castle Point. Seventy years

The paneled living room of Annandale.

later, in 1854, possession of the Hoboken property came full circle when Col. Stevens's youngest son, Edwin Augustus (1795–1868), patriarch of the Bernardsville Stevens clan, took as his second wife, Martha Bayard Dod, a descendent in the seventh generation of Anna Stuyvesant Bayard.

After the colonel's death, in 1838, title to the property passed to the family-controlled Hoboken Land and Improvement Company, one of the first corporations to be organized in New Jersey. Gradually, the family sold off property and helped develop Hoboken, which was incorporated as a city in 1855. It was the colonel's son, Edwin, who, in 1868, left an endowment and much of the land comprising the family's Castle Point estate for a "school of learning," which was established two years later as Stevens Institute of Technology, the world's first college devoted to engineering.

Col. John Stevens, who was both an inventor and entrepreneur, became interested in the use of steam power for transportation in the late 1780s when he witnessed John Fitch's experimental steamboat plying the Delaware River. The experience changed Stevens's life. Soon he designed a steam engine of his own with an improved vertical boiler. Looking for a means to protect his ideas, Stevens, in the early 1790s, was instrumental in getting Congress to enact the first United States patent laws, and he received one of the first patents to be issued. In 1804, several years before Robert Fulton achieved success with his steamboat, the *Clermont*, the colonel built the first successful twin-screw, propeller-driven, multitubular boiler vessel, the *Little Juliana*, which crossed the Hudson River. Unfortunately, his dreams of establishing a Hudson ferry service were stymied for a time by Fulton who had garnered a legal monopoly on Hudson River steam operations. Five years later, however, a larger and far more sophisticated craft, named the *Phoenix*, designed by the colonel and his son, Robert Livingston (1787–1856), became the first steamboat to successfully venture onto the open ocean when it traveled from Hoboken, along the New Jersey coast, around Cape May, and up the Delaware

River to Philadelphia, where it went into regular ferry service between that city and Trenton.

Col. Stevens's fertile mind also came up with ideas well beyond the use of steam power, including many that would not be carried out until many years after his death. In the late 1790s he helped design New York City's first water-supply system with mains made of hollowed-out pine logs; in the yellow fever epidemic of 1795, he suggested that the sick be quarantined on "floating stages" in the river beyond the wharf line, a precursor of floating hospitals; he ruminated on an idea that would later evolve into the internal-combustion engine; he envisioned a bridge over, and a vehicular tunnel under, the Hudson River; and in the War of 1812, he proposed the first ironclad craft with a revolving gun turret, similar to the *Monitor* and to a vessel designed by his son, Edwin, that would be constructed during the Civil War.

In 1812, five years before construction began on the Erie Canal, Col. Stevens began to promote his then-visionary idea of marrying steam power to railroads, publishing a well-reasoned treatise that the future of transportation lay with railways, not canals, which were then favored by the country's political and financial interests. Although in 1815 he received a charter—the first in America—to build a railroad from Trenton to New Brunswick, New Jersey, and eight years later obtained a similar charter to construct a railroad in Pennsylvania, he was not able to attract the necessary financial backing, and his grand idea languished until 1830.

In an effort to sway public opinion, the colonel, at age seventy-seven, and son Robert built a circular track in Hoboken in 1826 on which they ran a "steam carriage" they had designed and built. It was the first American-built steam locomotive and it chugged along at a then-breakneck speed of twelve miles per hour.

Finally, in 1830, the colonel's dreams were realized when his sons, Robert and Edwin, obtained a new charter for the Camden & Amboy Railroad to link Raritan Bay and

Opposite, above: House of Richard and Elsie Stevens, completed in 1900 and destroyed by fire on Armistice Day, November 11, 1918, which was also the couple's twenty-fifth wedding anniversary.

Opposite, below: House of Richard and Elsie Stevens.

the Delaware River. Robert soon sailed for England to purchase a suitable locomotive, the historic *John Bull*, which was to be the first truly efficient passenger locomotive in the United States. On the trip Robert designed the T-rail that came to be adopted as the universal form of track rail.

The impressive list of Robert Stevens's inventions in the fields of railroad and steamboat transportation included such things as the hook-headed railroad spike; the "cowcatcher," a protective grid of sloping bars affixed to the front of a locomotive to prevent derailments; and the more prosaic, but exceedingly practical, idea of driving wooden piles deep into a ferry-slip bottom so that when a boat nudges into them they yield and spring back, thus helping the boat to dock.

Colonel Stevens's other children also made important marks in life. His oldest son, John Cox (1785–1857), more a businessman than inventor, was an avid sailor. It was on his yacht that he and several friends organized the New York Yacht Club in 1844. Stevens was named the club's first commodore and the first clubhouse was built on Stevens family property in Hoboken. It was also John Cox Stevens who, with his brother Edwin, headed the syndicate that built the famous schooner *America* and sailed it to victory around the Isle of Wight in 1851, winning the cup and the event now known as the America's Cup.

Edwin, whose offspring constituted the family's Bernardsville branch, was, like his father and brother Robert, an inventor, but he was also an astute business-man who from an early age managed the family's Hobo-ken estate and other business interests. Edwin's own list of inventions included the "Stevens plow," a cast-iron plow with an ingeniously designed moldboard that kept dirt from sticking to it; the "closed fireroom" system of forced draft air that greatly increased a steam engine's efficiency; and the American vestibule-style railroad passenger car with center aisle and doors at each end. It was also Edwin who, in 1841, when hostilities with England again appeared likely, resurrected his father's idea of nearly

thirty years before to construct an ironclad naval vessel. Edwin took the basic idea and improved upon it, design-ing what came to be known as the *Stevens Battery*, a huge craft more than 400 feet long and forty-five feet wide, sheathed in four-and-a-half inches of iron. The massive ship was never finished because the Navy kept changing the specifications. Later, during the Civil War, Edwin built—this time at his own expense and to his own specifications—a smaller, 100-foot ironclad, the *Naugatuck,* which the Navy accepted and which fought alongside the famous *Monitor*.

The family's inventiveness did not end with the gen-eration of Robert and Edwin Stevens. In the 1880s Edwin's son and namesake, Edwin Augustus Jr. (1858–1918), known to the family as "Ned," developed the double-ended, propeller-driven ferryboat, based on an idea first contem-plated by his grandfather, the colonel, as early as 1813. Although there had been double-ended paddle-wheel ferries before, propeller-driven boats could be stopped more quickly and efficiently. The challenge was to design a mechanism by which a single drive shaft running the length of the vessel, powered by a single engine, could be combined with the ability to load vehicles at both ends as well as be shifted into reverse quickly. The first ferry to use Edwin Jr.'s technology, the *Bergen*, effectively spelled the end for paddle-wheel ferries and became the standard design for vehicle ferries in use to this day.

In the late 1800s four children and several grandchil-dren of Edwin Stevens Sr. settled in Bernardsville, where they built summer residences. Robert Livingston Stevens (1864–1907) was the first to arrive, in 1891, buying 200 mountaintop acres. Although records of the George B. Post architectural firm suggest that Robert may have first lived in an existing house that William Stone Post altered and enlarged, newspaper accounts indicate that construc-tion on Robert's new house began soon after he acquired the land. The new home was a large fieldstone and shingle structure designed by Charles Edwards, an architect from

Opposite: Residence of Col. Edwin A. ("Ned") and Emily Stevens, later owned by Stevens relatives, the Hammond and Fenwick families. The aerial view was taken sometime before 1949 and before much of the fifty-room house was demolished.

Opposite, below right: Residence of Ned and Emily Stevens, as built circa 1896. The house was enlarged and altered by two subsequent owners, J. Magee Ellsworth and Ogden Hammond, then largely torn down circa 1949 by Hammond's daughter, Millicent Fenwick.

Opposite, below left: Originally the library wing, this was the only portion of the original house that remained after Millicent Fenwick had most of the house torn down circa 1949. It was remodeled for her by local architect James S. Jones.

Ned and Emily Stevens's second Bernardsville house, the former Anderson family homestead, which they owned from 1911 to 1925.

Paterson, New Jersey. About twenty-five years later the New York architectural firm of Lord, Hewlett & Tallant was commissioned by Stevens's widow to make alterations to the house and grounds to conform with the original design. Robert named his estate *Annandale*.

Robert soon convinced his brothers, Ned and Richard (1868–1919), to build summer homes of their own. Ned bought nearly forty acres from Robert in 1896 and built an enormous cedar-shingled house with fifty rooms, said to be reminiscent of the summer resort hotels of the era with high ceilings and French doors. Richard bought about sixteen acres near his brothers from George B. Post in 1899 and the next year completed construction of his own large, gambrel-roofed home.

After the Stevenses' sister, Caroline Bayard Stevens (1859–1932), was divorced from her first husband, Archibald Alexander, in the mid-1890s, her brother, Robert, conveyed to her an interest in his Bernardsville property. In 1911, Robert and Richard built for Caroline a large, comfortable home, designed by the architectural firm of Delano & Aldrich.

The four houses built by the Stevens siblings met different fates. In 1904 the rambling, shingled mansion of Ned and Emily Contee Stevens was sold to John Magee and Elisabeth Van Rensselaer Ellsworth, who retained the New York architectural firm of Warren & Wetmore to

design alterations and an addition. Ned and Emily did not permanently leave the area, though; six years later, in 1911, they bought another property in Bernardsville, the old Anderson family homestead on what is now Anderson Hill Road, which Emily retained until 1925.

Only four years after acquiring Ned and Emily Stevens's original estate, the J. Magee Ellsworths sold it, in 1908, to the Stevenses' niece, Mary Picton Stevens, and her husband, financier and diplomat Ogden Haggerty Hammond. Mrs. Hammond died in the sinking of the steamship, *Lusitania,* in 1915, leaving a son, Ogden Jr., known as "Oggie," and two young daughters, Millicent and Mary. Ogden Hammond Sr., who was elected to the local council and the New Jersey Assembly, also served as ambassador to Spain from 1926 to 1929, during the term of President Calvin Coolidge. His legislative and diplomatic experience made a strong impression on Millicent Hammond, who later gained national recognition as a public servant under her married name, Fenwick.

Millicent Vernon Hammond Fenwick (1910–1992), who settled in the family home in Bernardsville, began a political career after a fourteen-year stint as a writer and editor at *Vogue* magazine. She became the first woman to be elected to the Bernardsville Borough Council, in 1958, and went on to serve in other positions in local and state government. In the mid-1970s she was elected to the

Gardens at the Delano & Aldrich-designed house of Caroline Stevens Alexander Wittpenn.

United States House of Representatives where she became known as the "conscience of Congress" and was a celebrity of sorts when she was used as the model for the aristocratic, pipe-smoking Lacey Davenport in the popular comic strip, *Doonesbury.* After leaving Congress, she was appointed ambassador to the United Nations Food and Agricultural Organization.

In 1949, unable to afford the upkeep on the family mansion, Fenwick reluctantly had three-quarters of the original house taken down, all but a library wing. Later, she recalled that "the beams screamed terribly when they were ripped apart." James Jones, a prominent local architect, was enlisted to help with the remodeling of the remaining wing. After Fenwick's death, the house became the property of her son, Hugh, who served nearly two terms as Bernardsville's mayor before his death in 2002.

The home built by Robert Stevens, who died in 1907 without a will, eventually passed into the hands of his daughter, the late Mary Stevens Baird. Baird, who shared her family's penchant for public service, was active in war relief efforts during World War II, and later championed the cause of prison reform, long a Stevens family issue. Like Fenwick, Baird had part of her home demolished for greater efficiency. Upon her death, she willed it to Stevens Institute for use as a retreat and conference center. The institute sold it in the 1990s.

The home built by Richard and Elsie Stevens was destroyed by fire on November 11, 1918—notably, the day was both the first Armistice Day and the twenty-fifth anniversary of their marriage. Part of the land was sold to Richard's half-niece, Esther Maria Lewis, after the death of her husband, Charles M. Chapin, in 1932. Esther, known as Lili, a granddaughter of Edwin A. Stevens Sr. by his first wife, sold her marital home, *Dunleith,* and had a smaller summer cottage built on the land formerly owned by Richard Stevens. She named her new home *Sunset House,* which was sited across the road from *Dunleith.*

Caroline Bayard Stevens Alexander remained in the house her brothers built for her. In 1915 she was remarried, to H. Otto Wittpenn, who was thirteen years her junior. Wittpenn served three terms as mayor of Jersey City and then was appointed Naval Officer of the Port of New York by President Wilson. The Wittpenn estate eventually became the property of Caroline's grandson by her first marriage, Archibald Alexander III, a lawyer who had a distinguished career. He served as treasurer of the state of New Jersey, undersecretary of the Army under President Truman, and assistant director of the United States Arms Control and Disarmament Agency. After the deaths of Alexander and his wife, Jean, the home passed out of family ownership in the 1980s.

*Right and below:
The house of Caroline Stevens
Alexander Wittpenn was
designed in 1911 and remained in
her family until the 1980s.*

BLYTHEWOOD/
FAIRCOURT

LIKE SO MANY successful American merchants at
the turn of the twentieth century, Henry Rudolph
Kunhardt (1860–1923) was the son and namesake of a
German immigrant. Kunhardt's father, who was born in
Hamburg, came to California in 1848 from South America and formed a mercantile and banking business in San
Francisco. In 1850 he moved to New York City where he
established the steamship agent and import/export firm
Kunhardt & Company. Kunhardt, the son, was born at the
family's home on Staten Island. After attending private
schools in America and Europe, he was employed by Atlas
Steamship Company of New York. In 1882 he joined the
family company where he worked until his death. Kunhardt & Company was general agent of the Hamburg-
American Line for thirty-eight years, importing coffee,
cocoa, hides, and logwoods from South America while
exporting United States products to that continent.

In 1888 Kunhardt married Mabel Alethea Farnham,
whose father managed a wool mill in New York. The couple
lived in Staten Island until the mid-1890s when, following in
the footsteps of many affluent New Yorkers, they bought a
175-acre tract of land and built a residence on the Bernardsville mountain. The property, which came to include a farmhouse, barns, stables, coachman's house, and coach barns, was
purchased from Samuel S. Borrowe, a vice president and
director of the Equitable Life Assurance Society.

In 1897 the Kunhardts hired New York architect
Henry Rutgers Marshall to draw the plans for their new
home, while the noted landscape architecture firm of
Olmsted, Olmsted & Eliot was employed to design a pre-
liminary plan for the layout of the estate. John Charles
Olmsted, a partner in the firm and nephew of Frederick
Law Olmsted, was assisted by a local civil engineer from
Morristown, John Rowlett Brinley, who later designed
landscape elements on the estate, including the extensive
stone walls bordering the property.

Marshall, who was not only an architect, but also an
author and lecturer, served for many years as an influential
member of the New York Art Commission and directed
the Municipal Art Society. Among his notable designs were
Rudyard Kipling's Brattleboro, Vermont, residence; the
Storm King clubhouse at Cornwall, New York; buildings

at Bryn Mawr School in Baltimore and the Brearly School in New York; and the Voorhees Library at Rutgers University in New Jersey.

There were two long and winding private roads leading up to *Blythewood*, laid out by the Olmsted firm. Each entrance was flanked by wrought-iron gates and a stucco gatehouse. The longer of the roads, from the south, was two miles long and wound through grounds abounding in roses, arbors and hedges, through rocky ridges, and over brooks. Locals recall that on Sunday afternoons, townspeople enjoyed driving their buggies up the driveways to admire the flora, especially the cascades of rambling roses. Kunhardt and his neighbor, architect George B. Post, had a new road constructed between their properties—now known as Post-Kunhardt Road—to define their boundaries so that service entrances could be advantageously sited.

The Kunhardts acquired additional tracts of land, eventually amassing an estate of about 350 acres. In August 1914 the stables, cow barn, and wagon sheds, along with many of *Blythewood's* valuable trees, were destroyed by a fire that came within 150 feet of the main house.

As their three sons grew older, the Kunhardts spent more time at their New York City home. Eventually they stopped visiting *Blythewood* altogether. In 1916 a Bernardsville neighbor, Col. Anthony R. Kuser, bought the estate in what was reported to be the largest real estate deal in the area for many years. The transaction, which included about 250 acres, was thought to be worth at least $250,000.

The Kusers hired the architectural firm of Hoppin &

Koen to undertake substantial interior and exterior alterations to the house, which they renamed *Faircourt* after their previous home nearby. A wing and a courtyard were added and the utilities were modernized. The relatively simple *Blythewood* was transformed into an ornate *Faircourt* with a grand marble staircase, rooms and halls of marble flooring, a ballroom, stained-glass windows, and deeply carved moldings with gold leaf. Local Italian artisans created intricately detailed Rococo ceilings. The Kusers also hired the New York landscape architecture firm of Brinley & Holbrook—which the Kusers had worked with on their first home and which had worked for the Kunhardts—to carry out changes in the landscape design.

In 1918 the Kusers' son, Dryden, married Brooke Russell, later Astor, and initially the young couple lived at *Faircourt* with his parents. One night while asleep, Brooke, Dryden, and others in the house were chloroformed and Brooke's jewelry was stolen, including her engagement ring, which was slipped off her finger. The culprits were never found.

Although Brooke was awed by the grandiosity of her in-laws' lifestyle—a butler and three footmen in the dining room, four chauffeurs, and a servants' wing to accommodate sixteen in-house staff—an account of the interior of the house, written by Brooke in her 1980 memoir, *Footprints*, is disapproving:

The décor of the house was frightful, what Mother called Early Pullman. Stiff brocade armchairs with fringes around the bottom were scattered through the main rooms at such

a distance that it was almost impossible for conversation. The bedrooms were all "suites"—in other words identically matched wood furniture with Tiffany glass lamps by the bedside. Even I, young as I was, thought it very odd.

Col. Kuser, a keen naturalist and bird collector, was especially knowledgeable about pheasants, having underwritten a seminal research expedition to Asia to acquire more primary material on the bird. One of the rooms in *Faircourt*, known as the Pheasant Room, Brooke described thus:

> The ceiling was made up of polychrome squares with a different species of pheasant in each square; and along the entire length of one side of the room was a glass case filled with stuffed pheasants. These birds were assembled as though in their natural habitat, grazing and nesting among the snows and crags of Mount Kanchenjunga.

Col. Kuser died in 1929 at his Palm Beach estate, *Los Incas*. His body was returned to Bernardsville for his funeral, which was attended by two former governors, the ambassador to Spain, and numerous captains of business and industry. His wife, Susie, continued to live at *Faircourt* until her death in 1932. The Kusers' daughter, Cynthia Dryden Kuser (1910–1985), resided in the home for many years with her husbands, Theodore Wilhelm Herbst and, later, Arthur Hinkley Earle. After World War II, Cynthia served as a translator in refugee work in Europe, managed the Dryden Press in New York, and was active in cancer work in the United States and Europe. After Cynthia and Arthur Earle separated, she moved to Arizona where she owned and operated the Two Shoe Cattle Ranch near Phoenix. The Bernardsville estate was left in the care of the superintendent until 1961 when it was sold and subdivided, with the house retaining ten acres. Cynthia Kuser Earle died in Arizona in 1985.

Blythewood *was designed by Henry Rutgers Marshall and built for Henry and Mabel Kunhardt in 1897. After the property was sold to Anthony and Susie Kuser in 1916, the architectural firm of Hoppin & Koen designed extensive alterations and additions, including the dining room and adjacent porch with French doors. The Kusers renamed the estate* Faircourt, *after their previous home nearby.*

DENBROOKE

T HIS RAMBLING RESIDENCE on the Bernardsville mountain was the marital home of J. Dryden Kuser (c. 1897–1964) and his first wife, Brooke Russell, who later married Vincent Astor. Additions and alterations over the years have resulted in an eclectic style that owes much to the Classical Revival movement with its six-pillared, two-story portico and imposing pediment.

It was long assumed that *Denbrooke* was built by Dryden's father, Col. Anthony R. Kuser, as a wedding present for Dryden and Brooke, who married in 1919. But in her 1980 autobiography, *Footprints*, Brooke Astor recalled that at the time of her marriage, tenants occupied the house, which was then part of the Kusers' estate, *Faircourt.* It appears that the house was originally the residence of Euphemia and Samuel Borrowe who bought sizeable tracts of land on the Bernardsville mountain in the early 1880s. Samuel Borrowe was a vice president and director of the Equitable Life Assurance Society. In 1896 Euphemia Borrowe, by then a widow, sold the Borrowe home and twelve surrounding acres to Robert L. Stevens, a descendant of the prominent family of inventors and engineers from Hoboken, New Jersey, who already owned much acreage and a large house in the area. At the same time, Euphemia sold an adjoining 175-acre tract to Henry R. Kunhardt, on which he proceeded to build his estate, *Blythewood.* In 1910 Anthony R. Kuser acquired the old Borrowe house from the Stevens family and, six years later, bought an adjoining 230-acre tract that comprised the bulk of the Kunhardt estate, which he renamed *Faircourt,* the same name he had given his previous house down the road.

Although Brooke and Dryden's marriage lasted ten years, it was a mismatch from the start. Brooke was the only child of a Marine officer who was later named High Commissioner for Haiti. Her father's tours of duty took the family to many countries, and although she was exposed to a variety of cultures and places, her childhood was essentially sheltered. In her mid-teens, Brooke was invited to a commencement prom at Princeton University, where Dryden was a student. The two met and danced the night away. Dryden was beguiled by the shy girl who hung on his every word, and about a year later, in April 1919, when Brooke was seventeen, they were married. The cou-

ple made their home in Bernardsville, initially living with Dryden's parents at *Faircourt.*

Col. Kuser hoped Brooke and Dryden might choose to live at the family's 10,500-acre estate at High Point in Sussex County, New Jersey, but its isolation did not appeal to either of them. In 1922 Dryden and Brooke moved into the house they called *Denbrooke*—a conjunction of their names. It was a large house for the young couple: eight master bedrooms on the second floor, four on the third, and a twelve-room servants' wing. For Brooke, it was a relief to finally have her own house, but she was critical of its appointments, writing in *Footprints* that it would take a great deal of money to alter its many "ugly" features. "The wings on each side were done in a haphazard way with windows placed without design," she wrote. She recalled that it was "monstrously" furnished with the entire contents of a Newark townhouse that had been acquired at a sale. Dryden and Brooke hired New York architect A. Musgrave Hyde to make alterations to the house. A porch was torn down to allow natural light into the drawing room, a terrace leading out to the garden was added, and a balcony was built off the master bedroom.

Before long, the Kusers had a son, Anthony, known as Tony. Brooke immersed herself in the social life of the mountain colony—golf and tennis at the nearby Somerset Hills Country Club, bridge games, and *de rigueur* social functions such as the Hunt Ball and the autumn races on the Schley estate, *Froh Heim*, in Far Hills. She enjoyed driving through the pheasant and deer park that her in-laws kept, admiring what was said to be the world's finest collection of pheasants, Col. Kuser's lifelong passion. Brooke enthusiastically took to beagling, a sport that was rapidly gaining popularity in the area, hunting with George B. Post Jr.'s beagles as well as Richard V. N. Gambrill's Peapack pack. It was while on the hunting field that she met Charles "Buddie" Marshall, who eventually became her second husband.

Meanwhile, Dryden took a job with a Trenton pottery manufacturer, Lenox, and went into local politics. He became a Republican councilman in Bernardsville in 1922 and a New Jersey assemblyman in 1925. In 1930 he was elected a New Jersey state senator. Although never the

Dryden and Brooke Russell Kuser moved into Denbrooke in 1922 and carried out alterations designed by A. Musgrave Hyde. The original house is believed to have been built by Samuel Borrowe, who was an officer and director of the Equitable Life Assurance Society.

authority on birds that his father was, Dryden had an abiding interest in ornithology. As a child, he was taken on morning bird walks with trained ornithologists. In *Footprints*, Brooke recounts that lying in bed on a spring morning, Dryden could recognize seventy-eight bird songs. In 1913, at age sixteen, Dryden organized the Somerset Hills Bird Club and published its periodical, *The Oriole*. Years later he served as president of the New Jersey Audubon Society and wrote two books about birds, including *The Birds of Somerset Hills*. Towards the end of his life, he became a consultant for the New Jersey Department of Conservation and Economic Development.

In 1930, soon after Col. Kuser's death, Dryden and Brooke divorced. Dryden remarried and continued to live at *Denbrooke*—which he renamed *Longhedge*—with his sec-

ond wife, Vieva Fisher. This marriage was also dissolved, after which Vieva remained in the house. She lived on the property with her second husband, Lester Perrin, until 1946, when the house was sold.

After the death of her second husband, Buddie Marshall, Brooke married the wealthy philanthropist Vincent Astor. For many years following Vincent's death, in 1959, Brooke Astor administered the Vincent Astor Foundation, and she has sat on numerous boards, including the New York Public Library, the Metropolitan Museum of Art, and the Bronx Zoo. Dryden Kuser married three more times after Vieva Fisher. He died in 1964, when he was living in Sussex County near the wildlife preserve and bird sanctuary at High Point that his father had so loved and had donated to the state as a park more than forty years before.

UPTON PYNE

NOW JUST A MEMORY, the handsome stone mansion known as *Upton Pyne* once reigned as the crown jewel of one of the Bernardsville mountain colony's largest estates. It was built by Percy Rivington Pyne (1857–1929), a well-known New York financier and philanthropist, as a summer home for his family, which included his wife, the former Maud Howland, and their five children, Grafton Howland, Herbert Rivington, Mary, Percy Rivington Jr., and Meredith Howland.

Born to Percy R. Pyne Sr. and the former Albertina Shelton Taylor, Pyne was the grandson of Moses Taylor, a wealthy New York merchant and banker who established the import and shipping firm Moses Taylor & Company and later served as president of National City Bank of New York, a precursor to today's Citibank. Percy R. Pyne Sr., who was born and educated in England, came to the

Upton Pyne *occupied a hilltop site overlooking Ravine Lake. The estate grew to more than 500 acres.*

United States in 1835 and was employed by Moses Taylor's firm as a clerk. He became a partner in 1842 and remained there until he retired from active business in 1887, marrying his partner's daughter along the way, in 1855. Percy Sr. also succeeded his partner and father-in-law as president of National City Bank, upon the latter's death in 1882, and served in that capacity until 1891. The younger Percy Pyne's brother, Moses Taylor Pyne, was a major benefactor and trustee of Princeton University. His Princeton estate, *Drumthwacket,* is now the official residence of New Jersey's governor.

Percy R. Pyne graduated from Princeton then began working for National City Bank under his grandfather Taylor's tutelage. He never severed his connections to that bank, and was serving on its board of directors at the time of his death in 1929, the same year it became the largest commercial bank in the world. Throughout his long business career, Pyne was active in many corporations and companies, including the Delaware, Lackawanna & Western Railroad Company and the Cayuga & Susquehanna Railroad Company. He was also keenly interested in scientific research and served on the executive committees of the American Museum of Natural History and the New York Zoological Society. Pyne was a tireless and generous philanthropist, supporting countless charities and hospitals with his time and money.

After first renting a summer home in Bernardsville, Percy and Maud Pyne began to acquire land in the area, eventually amassing an estate of more than 500 acres. Built between 1899 and 1900, *Upton Pyne* was named after the English village that was home to Pyne's ancestors. The architect, James Lawrence Aspinwall of Renwick, Aspinwall & Owen, designed the three-story structure in the style of an English manor house. Featuring twenty main rooms and nine servants' rooms, *Upton Pyne* was constructed on a bluff above Ravine Lake.

Aspinwall, who was descended from an old and prosperous shipping and mercantile family that was related to Pyne's wife's family, joined the office of architect James Renwick Jr. in 1875. Renwick, one of the leading architects of his day, is most famous for having designed—with assistance from Aspinwall—both the Episcopal Grace Church, on Broadway at Tenth Street, and St. Patrick's Cathedral in New York City. Aspinwall became a member of the firm Renwick, Aspinwall & Russell in 1880 and is credited with the design of a number of buildings in New York, including the American Railway Express Building, the New York Infirmary for Women, the Society for the Prevention of Cruelty to Animals, and the Society for the Prevention of Cruelty to Children.

The Pynes selected James Leal Greenleaf to design *Upton Pyne's* landscape. Greenleaf, who taught and practiced civil engineering before turning to landscape design, got his first important landscape commission in the late 1890s, working with the Olmsted Brothers firm to lay out and design the extensive waterworks on the vast estate of James B. Duke near Somerville, New Jersey. In addition to *Upton Pyne,* Greenleaf's other estate commissions in the Somerset Hills included *Blairsden, Pembrook,* and *Wendover.*

Upton Pyne adjoined the property above Ravine Lake on which the original Somerset Hills Country Club, with its nine-hole golf course, was built in 1897–98. After the club moved to its present, larger course on the former Frederic P. Olcott estate in Bernardsville in 1918, most of the land that comprised the original club was purchased by Percy Pyne, and a house, named *Dogwood Hill,* was constructed

near the site of the original clubhouse for Pyne's eldest son, Grafton, and his wife. Several years later the house burned down, but was rebuilt. The house was later acquired by Mr. and Mrs. Charles Engelhard and renamed *Cragwood.*

In addition to *Upton Pyne,* the Pynes maintained a year-round residence in New York City. The town house that was built for them between 1906 and 1912 on Park Avenue remains an enduring example of neo-Federalist architecture. Designed principally by William Mitchell Kendall of McKim, Mead & White, the elegant details and balanced proportions of the building were duplicated by the architects who planned the adjacent buildings. The block is today considered to be among the city's finest examples of that architectural style.

Part of the original landscape designed by James Leal Greenleaf, whose work is also represented at several other area estates, including Blairsden, Pennbrook, *and* Wendover.

Recreational activities at Upton Pyne *included a grass tennis court and a cricket pitch.*

Pyne took a keen interest in all aspects of his country estate, particularly the horses, sheep, and Guernsey cattle, and he actively supervised the management of the extensive property. He expended large sums caring for his prize Guernseys, whose hooves were polished until they "gleamed like black gold," and he was said to ask his guests if they preferred champagne or milk from the estate, pointing out that the two beverages cost the same.

Pyne was respected and beloved in the community. He supported the Bernardsville school and was often seen giving local children rides in his roadster. Pyne was said to be the first estate owner in the area to give his employees pensions. He served on the first board of trustees of both the Somerset Hills Country Club and the Somerset Lake and Game Club, and on the Road and Improvement Society of Mine Mount, a residents' organization that financed the upkeep of local roads. Pyne died in 1929 at the age of seventy-two, having been in failing health since the sudden death of his son Meredith less than two years earlier.

Over the years, *Upton Pyne* was generously offered for the benefit of the community. In 1905 Pyne donated the use of his expansive lawns for a sport that was catching on in the United States—cricket—and soon two teams were organized, the Upton Pynes and the Bernardsville Eleven. During World War II, the mansion served the greater good of the nation in its role as Bernardsville's first aircraft-spotting station, with a purpose-built viewing platform affixed to the roof. The spotters—locals from all walks of life, from high school students to businessmen—were trained in aircraft identification and manned the sta-

tion round-the-clock. Later, the station was moved to the Bernardsville High School.

Mrs. Pyne's death, in 1952, marked the beginning of the end for the imposing stone mansion, which was expensive to heat and maintain. *Upton Pyne* won its first reprieve in 1956, when the Bernardsville public school system grew overcrowded and in need of new facilities. The Pynes' only daughter, Mary Pyne Filley Cutting, who had inherited the house, offered it for elementary school classes until a permanent school could be built. The school board accepted the offer, and children filled its rooms for four years in the late 1950s, while the Marion T. Bedwell Elementary School was being built. The house stood vacant for several years after that until a rose-grower from Madison, New Jersey, proposed to move his family there and maintain it in exchange for a nominal rent. That arrangement continued for almost five years, but the mansion once again stood empty after the family moved out.

Upton Pyne's last hurrah came in 1974 when Mrs. Cutting offered it as the site of the first Mansion in May, a designer showcase for the benefit of Morristown Memorial Hospital. Peapack-Gladstone landscape architect, John Charles Smith, who was selected to carry out the landscape design for the fund-raiser, spent six months and organized thirty-five subcontracting firms to execute the $250,000 job. The event was a success, but Mrs. Cutting realized afterward that there was no future for her childhood home, which had become a target for vandals. In what she described as "the most difficult decision of my life," Mrs. Cutting had *Upton Pyne* demolished in 1982.

The large Upton Pyne *estate featured many barns, staff cottages, and other outbuildings. The brick barns, shown above, were built in 1913 and were converted into a house twenty-five years later.*

Original stone barn group at Upton Pyne.

UPTON PYNE BRICK BARNS

WHEN AN ESTATE is truly built on a grand scale, even the stables are spacious and attractive enough to become a home. Such was the case with *Upton Pyne*'s brick barn complex, designed by New York architect and author Alfred Hopkins (1870–1941) and built around 1913 as part of Percy Rivington Pyne's sprawling estate.

The Pyne family—Percy, his wife, Maud, and their five children, all enthusiastic foxhunters with the Essex Fox Hounds—kept their horses and livestock at the barns for many years. Nearly a decade after Pyne's death in 1929, his widow decided to sell off that section of the estate. The barns and nearly 125 surrounding acres were bought in 1938 by New York investment banker William Armour and his wife, the former Dorothy Thacher.

Barn group designed by Alfred Hopkins and built circa 1913. East façade.

West façade, showing alterations designed by F. Burrall Hoffman Jr. circa 1938 to convert the former Pyne barn into a house for William and Dorothy Armour.

The Armours retained New York architect Francis Burrall Hoffman Jr. to design the renovations that would convert the barns into their home. Hoffman, who apprenticed with the prominent firm of Carrère & Hastings, started his best-known work when he was only twenty-nine: the *Villa Vizcaya* in Miami, the grand Italian Renaissance villa built between 1912 and 1916 for industrialist John Deering. Hoffman transformed the Armours' brick barns into a charming French Provincial-style residence of fourteen rooms. Among the home's unusual features was a dressing room and bath made from the circular bull barn.

Armour enjoyed his home for twenty years until he was killed by an automobile in New York City in 1958. The house was later sold to Walter Abbott Wood (c.1908–1993) and his wife. Col. Wood, who during World War II trained mountain troops and a commando unit in winter warfare, later served as military attaché to the United States Embassy in Canada. He was a geographer and explorer who made more than 100 ascents of mountains on four continents. From 1957 to 1967 he served as president of the American Geographical Society, followed by four years' service as president of the Explorers Club. His mother, Dorothy Harrison Wood Eustis, was the founder and longtime president of The Seeing Eye.

The Filleys retained a local architect, Eugene W. Mason,
to alter and enlarge the house in 1935.

UPTON PYNE
COTTAGE

FROM ITS HUMBLE BEGINNINGS as a coachman's quarters, the Bernardsville property known as *Upton Pyne Cottage* evolved into a gracious French country manor house that, for the better part of a century, was home to Mary Pyne Filley Cutting (1893–1994), one of the grandes dames of the Somerset Hills. Mary Pyne was the third child and only daughter of Maud Howland Pyne and Percy Rivington Pyne, a financier and philanthropist who was among the prominent New Yorkers of his era who were drawn to the Bernardsville mountain colony. Mary and her brothers spent their childhood summers at *Upton Pyne*, the family's 500-acre estate, where they enjoyed fox-hunting and other outdoor sports.

During World War I, Mrs. Cutting met her first husband, Lt. Col. Oliver Dwight Filley. The namesake and grandson of a former mayor of St. Louis, Filley received his preparatory education at the Rugby School in England and was graduated from Harvard. When World War I broke out, he went to England from South Africa, where he had been working in the mining industry, and obtained a military commission, earning the British Military Cross in 1915. Afterward, he transferred to the aviation section

The original coachman's cottage on the Pyne estate, designed by
William Stone Post and built circa 1902, was altered and enlarged
by Post, as shown below, circa 1922 as a house for Oliver Dwight
Filley and his wife, the former Mary Pyne.

An oblique view of the front façade shows the domed circular dining room with French doors, part of the 1935 alterations designed for the Filleys by architect Eugene W. Mason.

of the United States Army's Signal Corps. Oliver Filley and Mary Pyne married in December 1917, and her parents provided them with a small stone-and-shingle coachman's cottage that had been designed around 1902 by William Stone Post for the Pyne's estate. After extensive alterations and additions in the early 1920s, which were also designed by William Post, who was a partner in the firm of George B. Post & Sons that had been established by his father, the Filleys moved into their home and started a family. Daughter Mary was born in 1921 and son Oliver Jr. arrived in 1923.

In 1935 the cottage was tripled in size to about 15,000 square feet and converted to the style of an eighteenth-century French manor house, with stucco exterior, a slate roof, and a spectacular circular dining room. The architect was Eugene W. Mason of Bernardsville, who had earlier worked for the New York firm of Carrère & Hastings.

Oliver Filley Sr. died in 1961 and, two years later, his widow married Charles Suydam Cutting. A widower whose first wife had been Helen MacMahon Brady, the widow of financier James Cox Brady, Cutting had been a

friend of Mary Pyne's since childhood. He was a prominent tennis champion, naturalist, and explorer, going on a life-long series of expeditions to nearly every corner of the globe, most famously to Tibet where, in 1935, he was the first white Christian to enter the forbidden city of Lhasa. In 1966 Cutting and his wife added a graceful courtyard to *Upton Pyne Cottage*, designed by local architect James S. Jones.

Cutting died in 1972, and his wife continued to live in the house for another sixteen years. Through her years in Bernardsville, Mary Cutting maintained her passion for foxhunting and rode regularly with the Essex Fox Hounds—always sidesaddle, as she had been taught as a young woman—until the age of eighty-seven.

In 1988 Mrs. Cutting sold the house and the 100 remaining acres of the *Upton Pyne* estate to German film producer Bernd Schaefers. In 1991 Schaefers and his wife allowed the Women's Association of Morristown Memorial Hospital to use *Upton Pyne Cottage* as the setting for its Mansion in May decorating showcase fund-raiser.

Mary Pyne Filley Cutting died in 1994, at the age of 100, after a full and fascinating life.

*This and the two following pages show
Upton Pyne Cottage as decorated by
Mary Pyne Filley Cutting.*

Domed, circular dining room, added in 1935.

Library. The painting over the mantel is a winter scene by Anna Mary Robertson Moses, better known as "Grandma Moses."

Sitting room.

Drawing room. The unfinished painting over the mantel is by William Draper of Oliver Dwight Filley Jr., son of Mary Pyne Filley Cutting.

Living room. The painting over the couch is of Maud Howland Pyne, Mrs. Cutting's mother, by British artist Charles H. Shannon, painted circa 1900.

GREEN GABLES

GREEN GABLES is the whimsical name given years ago by a young girl to a magnificent Bernardsville mountain home with a distinctive green glazed-tile roof. The estate was originally named *Baricross*, a combination of the surnames of the couple—Leonie de Bary (1873–1928) and George Dillwyn Cross (1869–1936)—for whom it was built.

Leonie de Bary was the daughter of Augusta Cecil and Adolphe de Bary. Leonie's father was a wealthy wine importer who worked for the firm established by his father, Frederick. Frederick de Bary, who was descended from a noble Huguenot family that emigrated from France to Germany after the revocation of the Edict of Nantes, came to New York in 1851 as the sole agent for the French champagne house of G. H. Mumm & Company. In addition to his importing business—Frederick de Bary & Company—he established the de Bary steamship line and developed a 3,000-acre estate of orange groves on Lake Monroe in Florida where he built a sumptuous home—*de Bary Hall*—and entertained lavishly, presidents Grant and Cleveland numbering among his guests.

George Cross worked for Frederick de Bary & Company until the firm's dissolution, after which he became an insurance and investment broker. In 1903, two years after their marriage, George and Leonie Cross bought eighty-three acres in the Mine Mountain section of Bernardsville from Thomas Douglass. The land had been part of the Douglass family farm since the middle of the nineteenth century and encompassed the site of the mine from which the mountain got its name. The Crosses hired New York architect Grosvenor Atterbury to design their thirty-room fieldstone manor home, which was completed in 1905. *Baricross* contained many luxurious features, including a private balcony off the master bedroom, a silver safe in the dining room, a wine cellar, a hand-operated elevator, a stained-glass rendering of the de Bary coat of arms set into the windows of the trophy room, and three-foot-thick exterior walls. The estate also featured a swimming pool, log cabin bathhouse, stable, tennis court, formal gardens, and an icehouse.

The Crosses, who had no children, lived at *Baricross* for nearly twenty-five years. George Cross became the first mayor of Bernardsville, in 1924, upon its incorporation as an independent borough after withdrawing from Bernards Township. Leonie Cross died unexpectedly in 1928 during a trip to her father's Florida estate, and although George continued to serve as mayor until 1930, he did not reside at *Baricross* after his wife's death. He died of a heart attack in 1936 at the age of sixty-seven, and the estate was subsequently sold to August and Elizabeth Ammon Hummel.

August Hummel (1890–1959) was the founder of the Hummel Chemical Company of New York, which was established in 1916 to process lanolin into cosmetic and health products and later grew to specialize in munitions and pyrotechnics. A skilled chemist, August Hummel was

born in Germany and educated there and in England before coming to the United States on a scholarship from Pratt Institute with sixty dollars in his pocket. Mrs. Hummel was the daughter of German industrialist Henri Ammon, who headed the German Red Cross for the state of Bavaria. The Hummels, who became naturalized American citizens, had three children: Karla, Ellen, and Frank. It was Ellen who renamed the estate *Green Gables*.

The early years of the Hummel family's ownership of *Green Gables* were busy ones. Karla Hummel married Joseph B. Wiley in an elegant ceremony at the estate six weeks before the December 1941 attack on Pearl Harbor. Ellen met her future husband, Marine Lt. James M. Vreeland,

Architect Grosvenor Atterbury designed Green Gables—*originally named* Baricross—*which was completed in 1905. Atterbury also designed* Hillandale*, the Peapack–Gladstone residence of George R. and Katherine Kunhardt Mosle (see page 200).*

in 1942, and family lore has it that he tried to impress the Hummels by flying low over *Green Gables* while waving from an open-cockpit airplane. Ellen and Elizabeth Hummel later recalled being terrified that Vreeland would fall out, while August Hummel was more concerned about the chimneys. Frank Hummel joined the Marines and served in the Pacific theater during the war. The Hummel Chemical Company also assisted in the war effort, at one point receiving a congratulatory telegraph from the State Department for supplying the chemicals used in an air raid over Tokyo. On the home front, Mrs. Hummel was active with the Bernardsville Red Cross.

After the war, the Hummels began collecting paint-ings and artwork under the guidance of the well-known European art historian Dr. Elizabeth Doppler. The Hummels filled *Green Gables* with many priceless pieces, including a Rubens. They also entertained many notable guests, including actress Luise Rainer, who starred in the movie version of Pearl Buck's *The Good Earth*.

BRUSHWOOD

BRUSHWOOD was a quintessential turn-of-the-century Bernardsville mountain estate. The thirty-room fieldstone mansion accented with white Ionic columns included more than 100 acres of gently rolling terrain surrounding spectacular gardens. It was designed by New York architect Charles Alling Gifford (1860–1937), who is perhaps most famous for designing the Mt. Washington Hotel in New Hampshire and the "New Jersey" buildings at the 1893 Columbian Exposition in Chicago and the 1904 World's Fair in St. Louis. The 16,000-square-foot main house was completed in 1904 on land acquired by Alice Isabel Ballantine Young (1874–1949) and her husband, Henry Young Jr. (1871–1944).

A portion of the *Brushwood* estate came from landholdings acquired from the estate of Alice Young's father, John Holme Ballantine (1834–1895). Alice Young's parents' substantial *Crowndale* estate was located across the road. Local legend has it that 100 acres were given to Alice Isabel as a wedding present, but records show that *Brushwood*'s initial twenty-three-acre tract was purchased by the couple from the Somerset Land Company, a corporation formed by Robert Seney and others in 1894 to acquire the more than 1,000-acre estate of Seney's father, George I. Seney, who died the year before. The Somerset Land Company, which soon became controlled by brothers Grant and Evander Schley, was the first large-scale land-development enterprise in the Somerset Hills.

The marriage of Alice Isabel Ballantine and Henry Young Jr. in 1899 united two of Newark's most illustrious families. Henry Young Sr. was a lawyer, assistant United States district attorney, counsel for the city of Newark, and Essex County prosecutor. The Ballantine family founded Newark's P. Ballantine & Sons brewery with its distinctive trademark of three interlocking rings, signifying purity, body, and flavor.

Henry Young Jr. carried on the family tradition of a career in the legal field. He was graduated from Princeton University, studied law with his father, and was admitted to the New Jersey bar. In addition to his legal work, Young was a director of the Howard Savings Institution and the National Newark & Essex Banking Company. He was

elected to the New Jersey state legislature in 1907, serving two terms.

Alice Isabel Ballantine Young was an heir to the brewing business established by her grandfather, Peter Hood Ballantine, in the early 1830s in Troy, New York, and re-established in Newark ten years later. Alice's father assumed the presidency of the company after his father's death in 1883 and raised his family in their opulent three-story, red-brick mansion located at 43 Washington Street in Newark. The Ballantines also spent leisure time in Bernardsville at the family's *Crowndale* estate.

Alice and Henry Young had four children: Henry, John, Rodney, and Alice. The family split their time between the Ballantine's stately Newark mansion—now part of the Newark Museum—and *Brushwood*, which was built as a summer residence. The Youngs' four children went on to lead interesting and different lives: Henry Jr. became an attorney, New Jersey assemblyman, and sheriff of Essex County; John maintained ties to Bernardsville for many years, even working on the committee that wrote a local history, *Among the Blue Hills;* Rodney became a renowned archaeologist at the University of Pennsylvania and for nearly a quarter century led the group excavating

an ancient Phrygian city in Turkey, which led to the unearthing of a palace said to have been that of King Gordianus IV and his son, King Midas, of the legendary golden touch; and Alice married Richard Vliet Lindabury Jr., the son and namesake of the prominent lawyer and owner of *Meadow Brook Farm* in Bernardsville, who taught at Princeton University and served as an editor at *The New York Herald Tribune* and president of the Poetry Society of America.

Brushwood's picturesque hilltop setting was a perfect site for the estate, which included cottages, stables, a stone garage, a pump house, and a children's playhouse. The Youngs, who were passionate about gardening, added unusual specimen plantings and imported trees they found in their travels. The neoclassical design of the garden was said to be the result of Henry Young's interest in Greek and Latin culture.

The estate was landscaped by the New York firm of Brinley & Holbrook. The firm's senior partner, John Rowlett Brinley, who was from Morristown, was responsible for the landscape design of a number of estates in the Somerset Hills and Morristown area. A staff of ten gardeners tended to the grounds and greenhouses. Teatime on the

veranda was served against a backdrop of potted flowers, plants, and large tubs containing bay trees. Colorful blooming fuchsia spilled from the roof on both sides of the columned portico, and the mansion's rooms were decorated with fresh flowers grown on the estate.

A granddaughter of Alice Young recounted many happy times at *Brushwood* in a 1988 article in the *Bernardsville News*. Ethel "Duckie" Young Ritchie spent many summers there with her paternal grandparents during the 1930s and 1940s. Recalling a clandestine mission in which she and her brother and sister crept into their grandmother's room, she said, "we got into Granny's closet and stole her secret stash of chocolates. They always tasted of mothballs." She remembered playing cards with the Episcopal bishop of Newark on the living room floor, riding in the dumbwaiter, climbing onto the third-story roof, and applying makeup to marble statues. On one occasion, the grandchildren pulled a fire hose across the attic floor, carried it downstairs, and turned it on. Ritchie did not remember being disciplined for the incident, just her grandmother replacing the leaky hose. "I don't know why we weren't punished," she recalled, "Granny wasn't particularly indulgent. She had a look

that would stop us in our tracks. We called it her Medusa look." Aside from the mischievous activities of the children, life at *Brushwood* was fairly quiet, Ritchie reported. "Tea was served every day at five, either outside on the terrace or on the porch," she said.

Known for their philanthropy, Henry and Alice Young supported many charitable and progressive causes. Booker T. Washington visited the Youngs' house in Newark, and Alice Young was an advocate of Margaret Sanger, founder of Planned Parenthood. Henry Young was an honorary chairman of the Newark chapter of the American Red Cross, trustee of the Newark Museum, and served on the Newark Board of Education as a member and president in the 1920s and 1930s. An enthusiastic lover of the classics, he was president of the Carteret Book Club of Newark.

Henry Young died in 1944 at the age of seventy-two, and Alice passed away five years later. *Brushwood* remained in the Young family until 1951, when the house and twelve surrounding acres were purchased by Louis Bancel Warren, a senior partner in the New York law firm of Kelley, Drye & Warren, and his wife, the former Rosalie Watson, whose father founded the brokerage firm of Watson-

Armstrong & Company. The Warrens lived at *Brushwood* for thirty-five years and reportedly never changed the green carpet in the upstairs hall, where it was trod upon for eighty-four years. Some of the original wallpaper was still intact in the late 1980s.

Warren was recognized by the Vatican for his work promoting Roman Catholic education in the United States and England. He was a member of the Cardinal's Committee for Education in the Archdiocese of New York and was made a Knight Commander of the Order of St. Gregory the Great by the Vatican in 1957. Warren was a director of the Chrysler Corporation from 1957 to 1976 and was involved in restructuring the corporation and helping to recruit Lee Iacocca, who had been president of the Ford Motor Company, as chairman. Warren also

established the American Ditchley Foundation to address matters affecting the United States and Britain, and was a founder of the Lutèce Foundation to promote ties between art patrons in America and France. Among his many honors, Warren was awarded the honorary title of Commander of the Order of the British Empire and Chevalier of the French Legion of Honor.

When Warren died in 1986, he bequeathed *Brushwood* to Morristown Memorial Hospital. Two years later, the estate was transformed into a designer showcase for Mansion in May, a fund-raising benefit for the hospital. The home was sold by the hospital that same year, and changed hands once again in 1993. The current owners have done much to restore the residence to its former splendor.

BERGLOTTE

No longer standing, the imposing Bernardsville residence named *Berglotte* was built sometime between 1901 and 1905 as a summer residence for prominent attorney Frank Bergen (1851–1934) and his family. The estate name may have been derived from the family's Norwegian surname and the name of Bergen's eccentric and musical daughter, Charlotte.

Born in Hillsborough Township in New Jersey's Somerset County, Frank Bergen attended public school and went on to read for the law with his uncle, prominent Somerville, New Jersey, attorney Isaiah N. Dilts. Bergen was admitted to the bar in 1873 and three years later was named a counsellor. For more than twenty years, Bergen was associated with the Elizabeth, New Jersey, law firm of Cross, Bergen & Noe, establishing a reputation as a formidable corporate lawyer. While practicing in Elizabeth, he was elected city attorney, an office he held for many years, fighting some of that city's greatest legal battles, framing important legislation, and restructuring the city's debt.

In 1903 Bergen was appointed general counsel of the Public Service Corporation of New Jersey. He retired from private practice and devoted the rest of his life to the public sector, becoming an authority on water supply issues. Bergen served as president of the Plainfield-Union Water Company, Elizabethtown Water Company, and the Middlesex Water Company. On two occasions Bergen was offered, but declined, appointments to the judiciary: in 1899 as chief justice for Puerto Rico and in 1906 as a New Jersey Supreme Court justice.

Bergen wrote many essays and speeches, a number of them on water issues, which were collected into two published volumes. Among his many pro bono activities was his involvement with the Washington Association of New Jersey, of which he served as president. In that capacity he oversaw the establishment of the Morristown National Historical Park, in 1933, which included the transfer from the association to the federal government of the Ford mansion, George Washington's Morristown headquarters. Bergen was also a founding member and president of Bernardsville's board of trade, established in 1916. For many years he was also a trustee and vice president of the New Jersey Historical Society.

Berglotte *was designed by Hoppin, Koen & Huntington and built between 1901 and 1905. The firm also designed* The Mount, *Edith Wharton's house in Lenox, Massachusetts, and carried out extensive alterations and additions to* Blythewood / Faircourt, *the Bernardsville residence of Anthony R. Kuser.*

In 1887 Bergen married Lydia Gardiner, a soprano who once sang a command performance before Queen Victoria. Lydia was a descendant of the family that has owned Gardiners Island off East Hampton, Long Island, since 1639. The couple had two sons—both of whom died prematurely, one in infancy and one in a car accident—and a daughter, Charlotte. Charlotte, inherited her mother's musicality, becoming completely absorbed by the cello from a young age. She once said, "I spent thirty-five years of my life in a little room on the third floor playing the cello." In the 1930s Charlotte acquired a rare 1701 Stradivarius violoncello—known to collectors as the Servais—which she later donated to the Smithsonian Institution.

Berglotte was designed by the New York architectural firm of Hoppin, Koen & Huntington, which also designed houses in Newport and the Hudson River Valley as well as several public buildings in New York City, including the elegant, domed Renaissance Revival police headquarters on Centre Street, which was converted to apartments in the 1980s. One of the firm's best-known residential commissions was author Edith Wharton's Lenox, Massachusetts, home, *The Mount.*

Bergen built his house on a hill adjacent to *Meadow Brook Farm*, the property of another prominent attorney, Richard V. Lindabury, with whom Bergen worked on several legal briefs. *Berglotte* was a magnificent glazed white-brick structure of French neoclassical design. Small tiles were embedded in the surface of the Corinthian columns of the grand two-story portico. The estate comprised more than 200 acres and was operated as a working farm.

After Bergen's death in 1934, his daughter took over the management of the property, and became heavily involved in its operation. She ventured into dairy farming, producing milk that she claimed was the cleanest in New Jersey. Charlotte liked to operate her ten-ton tractor, which she called Hercules, for long hours into the night. An eccentric and a recluse, whose diet was said to consist largely of shredded wheat and vanilla ice cream, Charlotte loved baseball so much that she had a baseball diamond built on her estate and invited local teams to play.

Years after the death of her mother in 1948, Charlotte renewed her passion for music and began directing a choir at a local Bernardsville church. This led to her presenting and conducting free concerts in New York City for ten years. Initially she leased Town Hall for the concerts, but towards the end of her life she rented Carnegie Hall several times a year, engaging the American Symphony Orchestra, which she conducted. Charlotte refused to charge a fee from the enthusiastic concertgoers who lined up to hear the works of Brahms, Beethoven, Mozart, and many other composers. Declaring that "music is too precious to sell," she said the concerts represented "the fulfillment of my life."

Charlotte died in 1982 at the age of eighty-four. Her will specified that the proceeds from the sale of *Berglotte* be used to set up a foundation for the arts in the name of her parents. Another beneficiary was the American Symphony Orchestra, to which she left $100,000. Before the estate sale, a team from Sotheby's discovered a pastel portrait, *Afternoon in the Park*, by the nineteenth-century American artist William Merritt Chase, which was valued then at $200,000, wrapped in sheets in a dusty crawl space in the attic. In a significant loss to Bernardsville's architectural heritage, *Berglotte* was severely damaged by fire, thought to be the work of vandals, in March 1984. It took fifty firefighters three hours to contain the blaze. The house was soon demolished and the estate was broken up for housing sites.

MEADOW BROOK FARM

Born a farmer's son in Peapack, New Jersey, Richard Vliet Lindabury (1850–1925) came from humble beginnings. As a child, he attended school only sporadically, because he was often needed on the family farm. Despite his irregular education, Lindabury's academic assets were noticed early on. When Richard was about twenty, a relative and former member of Congress, Alvah H. Clark of Somerville, New Jersey, took an interest in the young man's keen academic sense and offered to educate him in the field of law. A quick study, Richard was admitted to the bar in 1874 at the age of twenty-four.

With eighty-four dollars to his name, Lindabury opened a legal practice in Bound Brook and, four years later, moved his office to Elizabeth. Though involved in general practice for the next twenty years, Lindabury made a name for himself as a corporation attorney when,

in 1892, he successfully defended the Singer Manufacturing Company against a state tax from which the company believed it was exempt. This was the beginning of an illustrious career as corporation counsel representing such clients as the U.S. Steel Corporation, J. P. Morgan, and Prudential Life Insurance Company. In 1897 Lindabury moved his offices to Newark, where he founded the firm of Lindabury, Depue & Faulks.

In 1891 Lindabury began his land acquisition in Bernardsville, eventually acquiring a 600-acre estate on which he built a stone-and-stucco mansion on a slope above Mine Brook. Ten years later, the house was altered and enlarged by the George B. Post architectural firm, with son William Stone Post acting as lead architect for the commission. Lindabury named the estate *Meadow Brook Farm*, and it was by all accounts a great source of joy to

Cattle continue to roam the pastures of Meadow Brook Farm, *much as they have for nearly 115 years.*

Lindabury's stone-and-stucco mansion, built about 1891, was altered and enlarged ten years later by George B. Post's architectural firm.

him. It was a working farm, comprising all manner of livestock, including one of the country's finest herds of blooded Guernsey cattle.

Lindabury was a respected and much admired member of the local community, highly regarded by the many townspeople who worked on his farm. He created and donated Bernardsville's municipal park and gave free legal counsel to local clubs and organizations, drawing up the documents necessary to incorporate both the Ravine Association and the Somerset Hills Country Club. Lindabury was asked to run for governor of New Jersey, but declined, stating: "If I can earn the esteem and friendship of those about me in my home town and state, I will be pleased, and I only wish to be known as lawyer Lindabury."

In addition to his legal work, Lindabury was a director of the Prudential Life Insurance Company and U.S. Steel Corporation, a trustee of Stevens Institute of Technology, and a commissioner of the Palisades Interstate Park Commission, among other appointments. Although he never obtained a college education, he was given an honorary doctoral degree by Princeton University.

Lindabury married Lillie Van Saun, and the couple had three children. Their son, Richard V. Lindabury Jr., married Alice Ballantine Young, whose family built *Brushwood* on the Bernardsville mountain.

It has been said that Lindabury's greatest pleasure in his later years came from a regular morning ride through his and his neighbors' properties. It was shortly after one such ride that he was discovered dead on the side of the road, having been thrown from his horse. An autopsy revealed that he had suffered a stroke, but there are conflicting opinions which occurred first, the fall or the stroke.

Meadowbrook Inventions, the world's leading manufacturer and supplier of glitter, now operates on *Meadow Brook Farm*, which is also still a working farm that breeds cattle. The family-run company, established in 1934, provides glitter for the toy and cosmetics industries, greeting card and holiday-decoration companies, as well as boat manufacturers that use it for boat finishes. The company's factory is out of sight of passersby, who see only herds of Hereford cattle meandering around the lush green pastures where the meadow meets the brook, much as they have for nearly 115 years.

BRINKLOW / BROOKWOOD

IN 1904 George Campbell Smith (1858–1933) and his wife, Annie K. Schmertz Smith, acquired a forty-four-acre tract of land along what is now Anderson Hill Road and Chestnut Avenue in Bernardsville near the golf links of the Somerset Inn. The land, as well as an adjacent forty-one-acre parcel acquired by the Smiths in 1908, was purchased from the Somerset Land Company, a property-development firm controlled by brothers Grant B. and Evander H. Schley. The company had been organized by Robert Seney in 1894 to manage the Somerset Inn and develop the more than 1,000 acres of land that had been acquired from the estate of Robert's father, George I. Seney.

George Smith was a son of Francis Shubael Smith, one of the founders, along with Francis Scott Street, of the Street & Smith Publishing Company. Established in 1855, Street & Smith was said to have been the country's oldest magazine publishing company, and it remained in the control of the founding families for nearly 105 years until its sale to Condé Nast Publications Inc. in 1959. George Smith, who served as vice president and treasurer of the firm, and his brother, Ormond Gerald Smith, shared the management of the company following their father's death in 1887.

Street & Smith, which began as the publisher of *The New York Weekly Dispatch*, was long known as a "fiction factory," producing a wide variety of popular literature,

*Designed by New York architect Frank A. Moore in a "modified Elizabethan" style,
the stucco house was approximately 150 feet in length.*

including dime novels, pulp magazines, books in series for juveniles, fashion and homemaking magazines, comics, and adventure stories. The firm published thousands of books, and its list of periodicals once approached 100 titles. It gave up its pulp fiction work in the late 1940s to focus on its so-called "slick" magazines, such as *Mademoiselle* and *Charm*. Over the years the company had a large stable of authors, some of whose work was disguised by house pseudonyms. Many of them became highly respected literary figures, including O. Henry, Upton Sinclair, Horatio Alger Jr., Booth Tarkington, Bret Harte, Rudyard Kipling, Edith Wharton, and Theodore Dreiser. Street & Smith also became known as an "incubator" of

some of the country's greatest illustrators, including N. C. Wyeth, Norman Rockwell, Howard Chandler Christy, and Joseph Leyendecker.

To design their new home in Bernardsville, the Smiths retained New York architect Frank A. Moore, although Smith was said to have been actively involved in the design and layout of the estate. For the main residence, architect and client selected a style described as "modified Elizabethan," with stucco-covered walls and a moss-green tile roof. The commodious house, approximately 150 feet in length, featured a living room with a beamed ceiling, dark chestnut wainscoted walls, and a large Caen stone fireplace. The house had all of the usual accoutrements of

large estate houses of the period, such as eight master bedrooms, a billiard room, butler's pantry, silver safe, and a large service wing with servants' dining room and laundry. The house was surrounded by ten acres of lawn and two acres of flower and kitchen gardens, plus many acres of woodland and pasture. Other structures on the well-equipped estate included a farmer's cottage, coach house and stable, garage, cow barns, dairy, chicken houses, artesian well house, and ice house.

In 1910 the Smiths sold their home and sixty surrounding acres to Jane Nelson Bonbright and her husband, William Prescott Bonbright (1859–1927), who named the estate *Brinklow*.

William Bonbright, a Philadelphia native, had banking and mining interests in Colorado with his brothers, George and Irving, in the 1890s. Moving to New York in the early 1900s, they formed the New York investment bank of William P. Bonbright & Co., which later became Bonbright & Co. William served as president of the firm, which specialized in public utilities financings, until his resignation in 1920.

Shortly after purchasing *Brinklow*, the Bonbrights' daughter, Elizabeth, was married to Arthur Anderson Fowler, a sportsman, amateur artist, businessman, and writer, whose *nom de plume* was "Somerset." Arthur and Elizabeth Fowler's own estate, in nearby Peapack, New Jersey, was designed by the prominent New York architectural firm of Hewitt & Bottomley, with later alterations by Chester G.

Burden and Ogden Codman. Elizabeth died in 1918, leaving two children, Anderson Fowler, an artist, and Carol Fowler Bassett. The Bonbrights other child, Howard, a financier who lived in Grosse Pointe, Michigan, managed the Detroit office of William P. Bonbright & Co. for many years.

The summer after they acquired *Brinklow,* the Bonbrights hired a special train to bring all of the employees of the Bonbright firm's New York office to their new country estate for a picnic and games. The festivities included everything from baseball and track events, to more light-hearted activities such as pillow fights and potato races, with Mrs. Bonbright awarding prizes after each event. However, the Bonbrights tended to buck the usual practice of other area estate owners who spent summers in the Somerset Hills, preferring instead to travel to the lodge they owned on a salmon stream in Canada.

For services rendered in support of the Allies in World War I, the French government made William Bonbright a Chevalier of the Legion of Honor in 1919. The next year, the Bonbrights sold their Bernardsville estate and moved to England where William took over the management of the London branch of Bonbright & Co. Jane Bonbright died in 1924, followed by her husband's death in 1927.

Charles Anderson Dana (1881–1975) and his first wife, Agnes Ladson Dana, acquired the Bonbrights' sixty-acre property in 1920, renaming it *Brookwood.* Five years later, they acquired an adjoining twenty-four-acre parcel,

An estate cottage, which shared the same architectural style as the main house.

recreating the original eighty-five-acre estate that George and Annie Smith had acquired in the early 1900s.

Dana was a leading industrialist and philanthropist. He was named for his famous uncle who was one of the most influential and colorful newspapermen of the nineteenth century. The elder Charles A. Dana (1819–1897) got his start in journalism working as an assistant to Horace Greeley at the *New York Tribune,* where he actively supported Greeley and the paper's abolitionist stand. After serving as assistant secretary of war during the Civil War, Dana returned to New York and the newspaper business, becoming the owner and editor of *The Sun.*

The younger Charles Dana, who earned undergraduate and law degrees from Columbia University, practiced law for several years and served as an assistant prosecutor in the sensational 1907 trial of Harry K. Thaw for the murder of architect Stanford White. Dana, who was said to resemble President Theodore Roosevelt in appearance and lifestyle—to keep in shape, he served as a National Guard cavalryman and a cowhand in Mexico for several summers—began a political career, serving six years in the New York State Assembly, before entering the business world. For more than half a century, Dana headed the Spicer Manufacturing Corporation, which, in 1946, changed its name to the Dana Corporation, a leading automotive-parts manufacturer. During his career, he was also an officer or director of more than twenty companies, including Manufacturers Trust Company, the Fisk Rubber Company, Empire Trust Company, and several companies in England.

In the 1950s Dana established and endowed the Charles A. Dana Foundation, which today makes charitable grants primarily in the areas of science, health, and education. In recognition of the Dana Foundation's long-term financial support of the Sidney Farber Cancer Center, that organization changed its name, in 1983, to the Dana-Farber Cancer Institute. Today Dana-Farber is a principal teaching affiliate of Harvard Medical School and a federally designated Center for AIDS Research and comprehensive cancer treatment center.

Charles A. Dana and Agnes Ladson were married in 1912 in her hometown of Atlanta. They had two children, Charles A. Dana Jr., who was married three times, and Agnes Ladson Dana, who married Morgan Cowperthwaite Jr. at *Brookwood* in 1939. Charles and Agnes Dana were divorced in 1938. Agnes Dana continued to reside at *Brookwood* until her death in December 1958.

Brinklow / Brookwood was destroyed by fire in 1963, and the estate was later broken up for housing sites.

CRAIGMORE

A SOMEWHAT AUSTERE edifice with a stone exterior and turret, *Craigmore* reflected the Germanic roots of its one-time owner, Charles Engelhard (1867–1950). Born in Hanau, Germany, Engelhard worked in a bank in Paris and then as a jewelry salesman in London before coming to the United States in 1891, at the age of twenty-four, as an agent for W. C. Heraeus G.m.b.H. Platinum Works of Hanau. Engelhard's maternal grandfather founded the contracting firm Philip Holzmann & Company in Frankfurt-am-Main and built one of the first railroads in Germany, and his father, Julius, was a jeweler. In 1900 Engelhard married Emelia "Emy" Maria Canthal—also from Hanau—and six years later became a naturalized United States citizen. The couple had one son, Charles William Engelhard, who was born in 1917.

The large multinational corporation that would eventually become today's Engelhard Corporation was started by Charles Engelhard in 1902 when he acquired the Charles F. Croselmire Company in Newark, New Jersey. The next year, he founded the American Platinum Works and later acquired several companies, including Hanovia Chemical and Manufacturing Company. Over the course of Engelhard's career, his firm became the world's largest refiner and fabricator of platinum metals, gold, and silver; the leading producer of silver and silver alloys in mill forms; operator of the world's largest precious metals smelter, and a pioneer in the development of liquid gold for decorative applications. He ultimately headed an enterprise with operations in the United States, Canada, Japan, Brazil, Switzerland, Denmark, and Great Britain.

Charles and Emy Engelhard moved to Bernardsville in 1912, buying property from Susie Price Sterling Quatrebeau, on which stood the large stone house they would call *Craigmore*. The elaborate three-story mansion had twelve bedrooms and featured an elevator, a windowed greenhouse room with brick floors, seven fireplaces, and extensive hilltop views across the property and beyond. With nearly 15,000 square feet of living space, *Craigmore* easily accommodated staff members on the third floor, where a head-servant suite and five maids' bedrooms were located. In 1915 and again in 1922, the Engelhards retained the landscape architecture firm of Brinley & Holbrook—which knew the estate because it drew garden plans for the Quatrebeaus in 1909—to carry out redesigns and replantings of the estate's grounds.

Engelhard was active in the community, serving as a director of the Bernardsville National Bank in the 1930s, treasurer of the Bernards Library Association, and a warden of St. John-on-the-Mountain Episcopal Church.

During World War I, Engelhard was chief advisor to the War Industries Board on platinum dealing. However, because of his German ancestry and the dominant position of his companies in the precious metals industry, he was subject to sensational and transparently false allegations made on the floor of the United States Congress: that he had connections to Germany's platinum interests that had impeded America's war preparations.

Through his friendship with President Franklin D. Roosevelt, Engelhard became involved in Democratic politics, serving as a presidential elector from New Jersey in the 1936 and 1940 elections. He also supported Roosevelt's Warm Springs, Georgia, foundation for infantile paralysis. In 1943 Engelhard was nominated by New Jersey Governor Charles A. Edison to serve on the State Unemployment Compensation Commission, a position he held until 1946. He was also vice chairman and trustee of Stevens Institute of Technology in Hoboken, from which he received an honorary doctoral degree. Engelhard, who gave a number of scholarship grants-in-aid to the school, was named a life trustee several weeks before his death.

Craigmore was occupied by Engelhards until their deaths—Charles in 1950 at the age of eighty-three and Emy in 1973 at the age of ninety-six. Emy was remembered with great fondness as president of the Virginia Day Nursery Summer Home, which operated in Bernardsville during the summer months, hosting underprivileged children from the group's daycare center in New York. The home fell on hard times during the Great Depression and would have closed had it not been for the Engelhards' patronage.

As an adult, the Engelhards' son, Charles William, moved to his own Bernardsville mountain estate, which he named *Cragwood* and where he raised his family.

Tall Oaks *was originally named* Brick House *by the family that built it around 1909.*

TALL OAKS

Tommy Dorsey.

SWING ERA BANDLEADER Thomas Francis "Tommy" Dorsey (1905–1956) remains the defining resident of *Tall Oaks*. Dorsey, whose brother Jimmy was also a bandleader, owned the sprawling Georgian-style mansion in Bernardsville during the peak of his career, from 1935 to 1944. He moved to *Tall Oaks* with his first of three wives, Mildred "Toots" Kraft, and their two children, Patricia and Tommy. When Dorsey bought the twenty-one-acre estate, the eighteen-room residence had seven baths, eighteen fireplaces, and a stable with living quarters. It was built around 1909 by John and Sophia Degener, who named it simply *Brick House*, on land they purchased from Samuel S. Childs, a onetime New Jersey state senator.

Dorsey was known as "the sentimental gentleman of swing" for his expertise on the slide trombone. *Tall Oaks* was Dorsey's country retreat from his frequent nightclub appearances in New York. With a reputation as a gracious host who enjoyed a good party, he endorsed an open-door policy at *Tall Oaks*. One of the first things Dorsey did after acquiring the property was to make a large part of the third floor into a dormitory for visitors. He outfitted it with five showers, bunk beds with ship-style rope ladders, pinball machines, and an elaborate sound system.

After hours, musicians would retreat to the Blue Room on the third floor to sit at Dorsey's long blue bar lined with leather and chrome bar stools, drinking ale drafted from a wooden keg in the basement. Dorsey occasionally broadcast radio shows from his Blue Room or from the pool house. A hobby Dorsey shared with his children at *Tall Oaks* was electric miniature trains. The lower rooms of the mansion were covered with lengths of tiny tracks laid out with bridges, tunnels, stations, and switches.

During the time that Dorsey lived at *Tall Oaks*, his band included drummers Gene Krupa and Buddy Rich and vocalists Edith Wright and Connie Haines. Frank Sinatra joined the band in 1940. Celebrity visitors included Lana Turner and Jackie Gleason. "My father never came home unless he had twenty or thirty people with him," recalled his daughter, Patricia. "He hired a chef away from one of the big Chicago hotel restaurants. My mom would tell him 'thirty for breakfast.'"

Dorsey built a pool and pool house at *Tall Oaks* that was a replica of Bing Crosby's in Los Angeles, the only difference being that Dorsey requested an Olympic-size pool. Filling it with water turned out to be a daunting task. Few homeowners in Bernardsville had swimming pools in those days, and Dorsey discovered he did not have enough water to fill his. The problem was solved by his electrician, Irv Trimmer, who also happened to be the chief of the Bernardsville Fire Department. Trimmer called the firefighters in and had the pool filled using the company's hoses. Dorsey showed his gratitude by giving an impromptu party. After that, pool-filling parties were held annually, and Dorsey became so well liked by the fire department that he was made an honorary member. In 1939 Dorsey played a benefit concert in Bernardsville for the department, attended by 3,000 enthusiastic partygoers, under a huge tent brought to New Jersey from Canada.

Dorsey made other close ties with the community. His mother acquired property in nearby Far Hills, and his children attended local schools—Patricia went to Miss Gill's School and Tommy attended Mt. Kemble School, which later became Far Hills Country Day School. It was not unusual to see Dorsey leading the Bernards High School band at football games. He also loved baseball, and he and his musicians often played pickup games against area teams with Frank Sinatra as shortstop and Bunny Berrigan playing catcher, with a liquor bottle in his back pocket.

The wartime economy, with concert tours cut due to gas rationing, hit Dorsey hard. In 1944 he sold *Tall Oaks* and moved to a farm in Greenwich, Connecticut. He was only fifty-one when he died in 1956, apparently choking to death in his sleep.

Tall Oaks was sold again, in 1949, to the Ferrante family who remained there for nearly fifty years. The Ferrantes kept many of the original details intact, including a bathroom wallpapered with Dorsey's sheet music cut into the shape of the New York skyline. After the death of Mrs. Ferrante in 1996, the family auctioned off many of Dorsey's effects, including a five-foot mahogany sea captain's wheel, autographed pictures, and glassware from the bar. The Ferrantes sold the estate in 1998.

MENDHAM

Hilltop Church.

DEAN SAGE RESIDENCE

THE RAMBLING Shingle-style house built in 1904 once served as the centerpiece of the estate property owned by Dean Sage (1875–1943), a lawyer and philanthropist whose life was dedicated to improving the health, education, and welfare of others. Brooklyn-born Sage was a grandson of Henry W. Sage (1814–1897), a longtime trustee and one of the greatest early benefactors of Cornell University. Henry Sage made his fortune in the timber industry in the United States and Canada through his firm, Henry W. Sage & Company (later, the Sage Land & Lumber Company), and also served in the New York State Assembly.

Henry's son, Dean Sage Sr., carried on the family's lumber business but was better known as a bibliophile, author, and angler. A member of the Grolier Club, Dean Sage Sr. had a notable collection of nineteenth-century first editions and books on angling, one of which was a volume he wrote that is a collector's item to this day, *The Ristigouche and Its Salmon Fishing*. The Sage family long maintained a private fishing camp on the Ristigouche River in New Brunswick, Canada, where, coincidentally, both Dean Sage Sr. and Jr. died, forty-one years apart.

Dean Sage Jr., a graduate of Yale, gained a certain notoriety in the newspapers in 1900 during his final year at Harvard Law School by getting married and taking a week-long honeymoon in the middle of final exams. He married Anna Parker, the daughter of a lawyer and state senator from Albany, New York, Major General Amasa Junius Parker. After first practicing law with the New York firm of Simpson Thacher & Bartlett, Sage helped found, in 1906, the New York law firm that became Sage, Gray, Todd & Sims. He was in private practice his entire professional life, except for one year when he served as deputy assistant district attorney for New York County.

After first renting a home in Bernardsville—the Condict home on Claremont Road—Dean and Anna Sage bought a thirty-acre parcel of land from Edward T. H. Talmage in 1903 and the following year began construction

of their Mendham country home, also acquiring an additional sixty-four-acre tract of land. The Sages raised two daughters and a son in their new home. Their son, Dean, who also became a lawyer, was an amateur zoologist and led one of the first expeditions to China in search of the giant panda.

Although busy building a successful practice, Sage found time to devote to civic affairs. During World War I, he served in the New York office of the Army Transport Service and the real estate division of the Army's General Staff. In 1917 in the midst of his business and war efforts, he was appointed Mendham Borough's second mayor. Prior to that, he served for several years as president of the borough council and as councilman. Sage held a wide range of positions in public service. For years, he served as a director of the Commonwealth Fund and the Josiah Macy Jr. Foundation. The latter organization was established by Kate Macy Ladd, of *Natirar* in Peapack-Gladstone, in honor of her father. Sage was a trustee and chairman of the board of Atlanta University in Georgia, a pioneer institution of higher education for black students. He also served on the executive committee of the Prison Association of New York.

A highly respected and educated businessman holding, in addition to his earned degrees, honorary degrees from Yale and Columbia, Sage was named president of New York's Presbyterian Hospital in 1922. Two years later, he announced plans to build "the greatest medical center in the world," a collaborative project of the Presbyterian Hospital and Columbia University. In 1928 what has come to be known as the Columbia-Presbyterian Medical Center opened its doors at Broadway and 168th Street in Manhattan. The twenty-acre site had once been a baseball field for the New York Yankees when they were known as the Highlanders.

Dean was an avid fisherman and, like his father, a collector of books on angling. His sudden death, at the age of sixty-seven, occurred two years after the death of his wife.

The Shingle-style house of New York attorney Dean Sage
was built in 1904. Sage later became president of New
York's Presbyterian Hospital and oversaw the creation of
the Columbia-Presbyterian Medical Center in the 1920s.

ELLIS COURT

THE MENDHAM ESTATE once known as *Ellis Court*, and now home to the Sisters of Christian Charity, originally belonged to a family that was plagued by tragedy.

The estate, including a forty-seven-room mansion of eclectic stylistic influences, was built for prominent businessman Frederic Cromwell (1843–1914) around 1892. The original architect of the house is not known; however, the New York firm of Carrère & Hastings, which designed the New York Public Library among many other prestigious commissions, was retained by Cromwell in 1896 to carry out work on the estate. Guy Lowell's 1902 book, *American Gardens*, suggests that *Ellis Court*'s classical garden colonnade may have been designed by that firm.

Cromwell, who traced his lineage to the English Parlia-

mentarian Oliver Cromwell, devoted much attention to the design and care of his property. A *Town & Country* magazine article from 1903 describes his landscape efforts as a "marked success…he has made an Italian garden near the house, and, going further than most people, has embellished the banks without his walls with shrubs and hardy plants, which will make the roadsides fragrant and brilliant with color throughout the season."

At the time that the Cromwells were building their Mendham mansion, their youngest son, Ellis Bowman Cromwell, after whom the estate was named, died. Although local lore tells of Ellis, who was just seventeen, drowning in a lake on the property, his obituary in *The New York Times* reported that he died while visiting his uncle in Brooklyn.

A building list for McKim, Mead & White—the architects of New York's original Pennsylvania Station and one of the most prominent and influential architectural firms of the late-nineteenth and early-twentieth centuries—indicates that the firm's only known architectural commission in the Somerset Hills area was a rustic stone clock tower built by Frederic Cromwell on his estate in 1894. The clock tower, believed to have been a memorial to Ellis, was demolished in the late 1970s. The Cromwell monument at Greenwood Cemetery, in Brooklyn, was also designed by McKim, Mead & White, in 1910.

Cromwell was treasurer and trustee of the Mutual Life Insurance Company for more than twenty years and served as a director of several railway transportation firms, including the Morris & Essex Railroad in New Jersey. He was also a noted local philanthropist. In 1893 he funded a major expansion and renovation of Mendham's St. Marks Church, which included a new pipe organ.

Cromwell died of complications from Bright's disease in 1914 at the age of seventy-one, five years after the death of his wife, Esther Husted. Surviving them were four of their five children: Seymour Legrand, Mary Rebecca, and twin daughters Gladys Louise and Dorothea Katherine. In 1919, five years after their father's death, Gladys and Dorothea leapt off a ship shortly after its departure from Bordeaux, France, in a joint suicide. Having served as American Red Cross volunteers, the young women suffered extreme depression after leaving their frontline posts in France where they had spent several months working under stressful conditions within range of German gunfire and air raids.

Frederic and Esther's oldest son, Seymour L. Cromwell, who lived in an adjacent estate—*Cromwell Cottage*—with his wife, Agnes Whitney, moved into *Ellis Court* in the early 1920s. Several years later, Seymour was thrown from his horse and subsequently died. One year later, his widow and the surviving Cromwell heirs sold *Ellis Court* to the Sisters of Christian Charity, who now use it as a convent and the Villa Pauline retreat.

This rustic stone clock tower was designed by McKim, Mead & White in 1894, perhaps as a memorial to the Cromwells' son, Ellis, for whom the estate was named. The tower was demolished in the late 1970s.

The garden colonnade is believed to have been designed by architects Carrère & Hastings circa 1896.

SANDRELLAN

I T WAS 1945 when industrialist Merrell Kerby Saunders
(1909–1973) took in the splendor of Mendham's
rolling hillsides and mountain views and claimed the former Cromwell and Prentice estate for his own. Splitting
the tract of more than 100 acres with his brother, Robert,
Kerby Saunders retained for himself the portion of the
acreage that included the original country manor. He
christened it *Sandrellan*, Gaelic for "Saunders' Land," and
used the estate for farming and entertaining.

As a young man, Saunders worked for Willis Carrier,
the air-conditioning magnate, a connection that later
launched him into the air-conditioning contracting business with his own firm, Kerby Saunders Inc. Some of his
large-scale contracts were for work in the Pentagon, the
United Nations, Rockefeller Center, and the World Trade
Center. In the 1940s his firm worked with physicist
J. Robert Oppenheimer on the development of the first
atomic bomb during the Manhattan Project.

Saunders had many interests and a sharp business
mind. During a sojourn to France just before the Nazi
invasion, he learned about Charolais, a breed of striking
all-white cattle that produce more beef than the North
American black Angus. After the war, he returned to
France with some investment partners and brought the
first Charolais herd back to the United States. At the time,
each top-quality bull was worth about $100,000 and sev-
eral roamed his Mendham property.

Relatives describe Saunders, who was known to sleep
only three or four hours a night, as a bon vivant. He traveled frequently to fashionable Palm Beach, Southampton,
and Newport and socialized with the likes of Marjorie
Merriweather Post and Ernest Hemingway.

Although the Saunders's reign was perhaps the estate's
most colorful, the house itself dates back to the early years
of the twentieth century when it was built by Frederic
Cromwell, one of the area's largest property owners. It is
believed that Cromwell, whose neighboring estate was
called *Ellis Court*, built the house, that was originally known
as *Cromwell Cottage*, for his eldest son, Seymour Legrand
Cromwell (1871–1925). The house and more than 100
acres were conveyed to Seymour by his father in May
1914. Although the original architect of the house is not

known, undated records of the prominent New York architecture firm of Delano & Aldrich indicate that Seymour Cromwell retained that firm sometime during his nine-year ownership of the property to carry out alterations or additions.

The same month he acquired the property, Seymour Cromwell was named a governor of the New York Stock Exchange, and a month after that his father, a widower, died.

Seymour Cromwell built an illustrious career while at the exchange and was elected its president in 1921. He went on to serve in that position for a rare three consecutive terms. During his tenure, he organized a crusade against unscrupulous traders and supported reforms to protect the interests of smaller investors. His disdain for swindlers led him to become one of the founders of the nation's Better Business Bureau. Also active in charity and civic affairs, he was named an officer of the Legion of Honor by the French government for his work with French orphans.

Cromwell's wife, Agnes M. Whitney, a sister of New Jersey state senator Arthur Whitney and of Mary Stuart Whitney, the wife of Robert Livingston Stevens of the famous Hoboken family of inventors, was an independent woman. She was the first woman to serve on the New Jersey State Board of Education. She also sat on the New Jersey Hospital Board and was a founder and president of the Colony Club of New York

In 1923 Cromwell and his wife moved into his father's former residence, *Ellis Court*, and transferred title to *Cromwell Cottage* to Kate Harrison and John Hill Prentice, whose daughter, Caroline, married Cromwell's son, Frederic, the same year. The young couple and Caroline's parents spent summers at *Cromwell Cottage*. Just two years later, Seymour Cromwell died, at the age of fifty-four, after falling from his horse.

Under the Prentices' ownership, the estate took the name *Willowbrook*, and a road bordering the property took on the family's name as Prentice Lane. The grounds of the estate were redesigned for the Prentices by two famed landscape architects, Ellen Biddle Shipman and the Olmsted Brothers, the renowned firm established by Frederick Law Olmsted, one of the principal designers of New York's Central Park.

John H. Prentice was a prominent banker and broker with the firm Clark, Dodge & Company. His sister, Mary Bill Prentice, was married to Edward T. H. Talmage and lived on an adjoining estate, *Woodmere Farms*. John Prentice was an avid big-game hunter and brought back from central Africa a rare white rhino, now extinct, which he shot on an expedition. The rhino was donated to New York's American Museum of Natural History. Prentice was also a decorated war veteran, commissioned a major in World War I. He was injured by machine-gun fire during a battle in France and later cited for his bravery.

Prentice died in 1925. Kate and daughter Caroline, whose marriage to Frederic Cromwell lasted only two years, continued to use the property until Kate's death in 1941. Shortly thereafter, it was acquired by the Saunders brothers.

The steeple of Mendham's landmark Hilltop Church (see Appendix page 240) rises above the pond at Sandrellan. M. Kerby Saunders introduced the Charolais breed of cattle to the United States, and a herd once roamed his Mendham estate.

WOODMERE FARMS / TOLLEMACHE HOUSE

Distinguished by four towering white Doric columns at its entrance, the mansion once called *Tollemache House* was built in 1894–95 for Edward Taylor Hunt Talmage (1867–1922), a generous and much-admired man known for his three passions: the countryside, animals, and his home.

The Talmages named their house after the Norman spelling of the family name, Tollemache. The house was designed by the New York architectural firm of Lord, Hewlett & Hull, although local lore has mistakenly linked the famed architect Stanford White to the design.

Tollemache House was host to many glittering social events, and its guest books, which still survive, read like a directory of the era's notables from Park Avenue to Tuxedo Park. An unusual feature of the house was an underground kitchen, built away from the main house, in which the guests' coachmen and grooms could eat and rest.

Edward Talmage was the son of Dr. John Frelinghuysen Talmage, one of the best-known physicians in Brooklyn, and the former Margaret Hunt, also of Brooklyn, a daughter of a prominent and wealthy merchant, Wilson G. Hunt. The Talmage family emigrated from England to New England in the 1630s. One branch of the family soon settled in East Hampton, New York, and by the early 1700s a branch of that family had relocated to New Jersey, eventually establishing a family homestead, called *Mont Verd*, about a mile north of Somerville. It was at *Mont Verd* that Edward's father, John, was born in 1833. After receiving his medical degree, he settled in Brooklyn, where the family rose to prominence; one cousin, Rev. T. DeWitt Talmage, was a famous theologian, and another served as mayor of Brooklyn when it was a separate city.

Edward, who was born in Brooklyn, was a businessman, working first for the Delaware, Lackawanna & Western Railroad and later as a member of the New York Stock Exchange. In 1893 he married Mary Bill Prentice, also of Brooklyn, and the following year purchased about ninety acres of the Andrew Morton Ferris farm in Mendham. The Talmages built *Tollemache House* as a summer residence, reportedly spending about $40,000 on its construction. Eventually, the Talmages acquired an estate of nearly 400 acres which they called *Woodmere Farms*.

Although Talmage died at the relatively young age of fifty-five, he retired from active business early and spent the last years of his life with his wife and three children and with his much-loved animals. He was a fine horseman and was a highly regarded judge of saddle horses in shows throughout the region. Talmage's love of animals caused him to take the lead in establishing the first Bernardsville Horse Show in 1902, which featured sixteen classes of competition for saddle and harness horses as well as farm teams. Talmage and his party were an elegant sight as they arrived at the show in his large yellow four-in-hand coach, *Defiance*.

Talmage was beloved by his friends and employees. His October 1922 obituary in the *Bernardsville News* noted that "Mr. Talmage's devoted and almost life-long employees acted as pallbearers" at his funeral. His love of animals bespoke a gentle nature. The obituary continued, "…and while all domestic animals were his friends, his horses and dogs were his real companions."

Talmage's widow stayed on at *Woodmere Farms* after her husband's death. In early 1926 she had two wings removed, leaving the house with twelve rooms. The wings were used to construct another house on the estate. Mary Prentice Talmage was remarried in 1935 to William Reed Kirkland Taylor, a widower who was the senior partner in the New York brokerage firm of W. R. K. Taylor & Company. Taylor died a year later. The property was sold in 1946. Mary Prentice Taylor died in 1964.

In 1926 wings on both sides of the center core of the house (see below) were removed and used to construct another residence on the estate.

Tollemache House, *designed by Lord, Hewlett & Hull, was constructed in 1894–95. This image was taken shortly after the house was completed.*

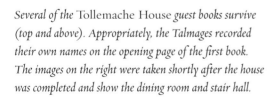

*Several of the Tollemache House guest books survive
(top and above). Appropriately, the Talmages recorded
their own names on the opening page of the first book.
The images on the right were taken shortly after the house
was completed and show the dining room and stair hall.*

*The rear façade of Oakdene before the 1990 fire
that destroyed much of the original structure.*

OAKDENE

IN 1892 NEW YORK BUSINESSMAN Charles W. Ide (1852–1903), a Brooklyn native, prominent member and president of the New York Cotton Exchange, and later a general partner in the cotton business of Weld & Neville, sought the tranquility of a country residence, purchasing land in Mendham. Ide served as a director of Home Life Insurance Company of New York and the Phenix National Bank and was president of the board of trustees of Long Island College Hospital, among other appointments. Ide's wife, Fannie Ogden Ide, was an author of children's books under the pen name, Ruth Ogden. She was also active in the anti-suffrage movement in the mid-1890s, protesting the "burdensome duty" to vote. In Mendham, the Ides built a timber-and-stone Tudor Revival-style mansion that has stood as a landmark in the region since its construction in the 1890s.

In October 1902 the Ides sold the property to William Scott Pyle. William Pyle and his brother, James Tolman Pyle, operated a soap company that their father, James Pyle, had established in New York in the mid-1800s. The company, later named the Pyle Pearline Company after its most important product, Pearline, once the most popular washing powder in the country, was acquired by the Procter & Gamble Company in 1914.

Under Pyle family ownership, which spanned twenty-two years, the estate was expanded into a thirty-six-room home and named *Oakdene*. William S. Pyle died in 1906 at the age of fifty, but his wife, Mary Vanderhoef Pyle, continued to maintain *Oakdene* as one of her residences. The Pyles, already a society name, gained publicity in 1919 when their daughter, Mary, a noted beauty, married the renowned American violinist Albert Spalding. During World War I, Spalding joined the armed forces, serving as a pilot in Italy where he was an aide to Fiorello H. LaGuardia, then a major in the American Air Service and years later the mayor of New York. Spalding was honored for his service in Italy with the Cross of the Italian Crown, the highest decoration conferred upon a foreign citizen.

The family captured headlines again in 1938 when the Pyles' son, Scott, a noted portrait and landscape painter, died at The Hague following an operation. Pyle had gone abroad to exhibit his work in Holland and Switzerland and had been instrumental in European experiments to make paint from plant colors.

Oakdene was closed for two years beginning in 1923, after which it was bought by the Oxford School for Boys. In 1928 New York lawyer Frederick E. Grant purchased the estate as a summer retreat. Grant was an attorney with the firm of Grant, Clark & Fox and represented many brewing concerns, the Brewers Board of Trade of New York and the New York State Brewers' Association. He was also president and general manager of the Interboro Mutual Indemnity Insurance Company at the time of his death in 1946.

Over several generations, the estate served as a church, a children's summer camp, and a religious-counseling center before reverting to use as a private residence. An effort to renovate the mansion in 1990 resulted in a fire that destroyed much of the original structure. It has since been carefully restored, returning it to its original magnificence.

Oakdene *was constructed in the early 1890s for Charles W. and Fannie Ogden Ide. It was sold to the William Scott Pyle family about ten years later.*

A leading Newark industrialist of the late 1800s, Edward Balbach Jr. and his wife, Julia, built Balbrook *in 1891–92.*

BALBROOK

A LEADING INDUSTRIALIST in the late 1800s, Edward Balbach Jr. (1839–1910) built the Mendham estate he called *Balbrook* in 1891–92. The fifteen-room mansion served as a summer retreat for the Balbach family, which also maintained residences in Newark and New York.

Balbach spent his childhood in Karlsruhe, in Baden-Wurttemberg, Germany, where his prominent family owned several estates and castles in the region. He was just eleven years old when, in 1850, he traveled to Newark, New Jersey, to join his father, Edward Sr., a chemist and metallurgist who had emigrated to America the previous year seeking business opportunities.

It was the "age of innovation," and Newark was a thriving port city and active industrial center, home to Thomas Edison's Ward Street factory and Peter Ballantine's Fulton Street brewery. While Edward Balbach Jr. attended school, his father started a precious-metal refining business that treated and processed jewelers' sweepings, which previously had been sent to Europe.

The company grew steadily, and once his studies were completed, the young Balbach joined the family business, demonstrating his father's technical ability. Edward Balbach & Son soon become a leader in precious-metal refining, attracting business from as far away as Mexico. The Balbachs brought to America carefully guarded European industrial practices and improved upon them. They introduced several desilverization processes, and the firm was said to rival the United States government in the production of gold and silver bars. After Edward Sr.'s death in 1890, the company was reorganized as Balbach Smelting and Refining Company, with son Edward as president. It continued to prosper under the younger Balbach who was not only a skilled metallurgist, but also a modest and charismatic personality. By the time of Edward Jr.'s death in 1910, the company employed about 500 workers and had annual revenues of $20 million.

Edward Balbach Jr. married Julia Anna Nenninger in 1869. They entertained lavishly at their Passaic Avenue residence in Newark, where they hosted some of the country's foremost leaders, including presidential candidate Grover Cleveland.

In 1908 a stone chapel was built in the woods on the *Balbrook* estate in memory of the Balbachs' grandson, Edward Randolph Jr., who died at birth in 1902. Originally named Edward Chapel, it is a replica of a small chapel in Bavaria that Mrs. Balbach once visited. Later renamed the Little Church in the Wildwood, it has hand-carved wooden pews on each side of the center aisle, a winding staircase leading to a small balcony, stained-glass windows, a crypt, and a marble fireplace.

The Balbach family influence reverberates through the generations. As industrialists intent on developing a pool of skilled workers, they were ardent supporters of, and financial contributors to, the Newark Board of Trade initiative, in 1881, to build a school for technology. This vision became a reality, and what is now known as the New Jersey Institute of Technology was born.

After Julia Balbach's death in 1933, the property was sold to Clinton Davidson, chairman of Fiduciary Counsel Inc., of New York.

Little Church in the Wildwood, a private chapel at Balbrook, *built in 1908 in memory of a grandson of Julia and Edward Balbach Jr.*

WENDOVER

Wendover was the Bernardsville mountain estate of self-described capitalist Walter Phelps Bliss (1870–1924). The thirty-nine-room mansion was one of the largest in the area, and in its heyday was the site of extravagant parties and equestrian events, attracting socialites from New York, Philadelphia, and Morristown. In his family memoir, *Momentary Bliss*, Walter Bliss Carnochan, a grandson of Walter Bliss, said the estate was named after the village in Buckinghamshire, England, from which his ancestors had emigrated to America in the early-seventeenth century.

Designed by New York architect Philip Hiss of Hiss & Weekes, *Wendover* was completed in 1905. Among the firm's commissions was the Gotham Hotel, now the Peninsula, on Fifth Avenue in New York. *Wendover*'s elaborate brick façade was ornamented with Roman pediments, balcony overlooks, circular and fan-topped windows, corbels, dentil molding, and cornices. The effect was that of an asymmetrical Georgian manor. Slit windows in the front of the house, modeled on those through which arrows would have been shot centuries ago, lent a resemblance to a medieval castle. A tile roof, with its more

Wendover was designed by the New York architectural firm of Hiss & Weekes and was completed in 1905. Shown below is the front entrance façade.

Rear façade.

den, several sunken flower gardens, and tennis courts that had wooden flooring for year-round play. One season they were converted into a skating rink. The estate also had one of the area's first swimming pools, installed in 1923.

The estate employed a staff of almost 125 farm workers and laborers, not counting domestic servants. Undoubtedly, the most famous of these workers was Rudolph Valentino, who was a gardener on the estate after emigrating from Italy—and before he became a famous screen idol.

The construction of *Wendover* and support of the Bliss family's lifestyle were financed by the legacy of George Bliss, Walter's father. The son of a carpenter from Northampton, Massachusetts, George Bliss was a self-made man. Financial circumstances forced him to leave school when he was eight to work on the family farm. As a teenager, he went to New Haven, Connecticut, where he worked in a dry-goods business, later moving to New York where he was a partner in a series of increasingly successful retail firms, the last being George Bliss & Company. In 1869 Bliss and former United States vice president and New York governor, Levi P. Morton, established the banking house of Morton, Bliss & Company, which primarily underwrote railroads. George Bliss's wealth reportedly reached $15 million. He died in 1896 at the age of eighty, one year before his son, Walter, wed Katharine Baldwin of Detroit, daughter of former Michigan governor Henry P. Baldwin.

Walter Phelps Bliss was a graduate of Yale University and Columbia Law School. Although he passed the New York State bar exam in 1896, he never practiced law, choosing instead to manage his father's business interests. Walter listed his occupation in *Who's Who* as "capitalist." Bliss was a director or trustee of nine insurance companies, four railroad companies, two banks, and a gas company. He was also involved in philanthropy, serving on the boards of schools, churches, and charities. But managing his Bernardsville estate, which included raising Ayrshire cattle, was one of his major interests. Bliss Carnochan described his grandfather in *Momentary Bliss*: "In life he was a formidable presence, with thin-rimmed glasses and thin hair, austere of demeanor, and looking much older in his official photographic portrait than his actual years."

At the age of only fifty-three, Bliss died of a stroke while riding the New York subway to his Broadway office. His wife, Katharine, lived for another forty years, sum-

Mediterranean feel, contrasted with the classic Georgian chimneys constructed of intricately laid brick.

The interior of *Wendover* was lavishly detailed with elements such as a twenty-foot-high entrance hall embellished with plaster rosettes, Doric columns with pineapple trim, and many Gothic and Renaissance influences. The main hall's paneled walls were reminiscent of Tudor England with dentil molding and floral carvings. A six-foot Renaissance marble fireplace and a French Renaissance curving staircase with massive carved oak banister were focal points of the main hall. There was a paneled ballroom with beamed ceilings, herringbone-patterned hardwood floors, and a cabinet that disguised the entrance to hidden stairs leading to an upper floor and wine cellar below.

The nearly 600-acre tract straddling Bernardsville and Mendham included formal gardens, a racetrack, a carriage house, brick horse stables, barns, greenhouses, a gashouse to manufacture acetylene gas for lighting, and what was known as the "boarding house" for estate workers. Over the years, two noted landscape architects had a hand in the design of the gardens and grounds—Ellen Biddle Shipman and James Leal Greenleaf. When *Wendover* was under construction, Bliss had mature trees brought up the mountain on horse-drawn wagons to cover what was mostly bare land on the mountaintop. The rear of the estate overlooked an extensive lawn, boxwood gar-

mering at *Wendover* and spending the balance of the year in New York. Walter and Katharine had four daughters: Ruth, Katharine, Sibyll, and Priscilla. Upon Katharine Bliss's death, the estate was sold and much of it became Roxiticus Golf Club. In 1979 the main house, which served as the clubhouse, was destroyed in a fire that killed the manager and his wife. The cause of the fire has never been determined.

The many outbuildings on the 600-acre estate included an elegant stable and coach barn (shown), farm barns, greenhouses, a gas house to manufacture acetylene gas for lighting, and a "boarding house" for some of the more than 125 estate workers.

Brookrace *was built in 1914 for Col. Richard Henry Williams Jr. on the 560-acre property that had recently been acquired by his father. Ernest Flagg designed the house, which features a sixteenth-century French stone fireplace that was removed from architect Stanford White's New York house.*

BROOKRACE

FIVE-HUNDRED-AND-SIXTY ACRES of wooded hills and meandering brooks acquired by Richard H. Williams Sr. beginning in 1912 provided a tranquil setting for the Mendham estate known as *Brookrace*, which was built in 1914 for Williams's son, Col. Richard Henry Williams Jr. (1884–1931). A decorated veteran of World War I, the younger Williams served as a lieutenant colonel in the purchasing division of the Federal Remount Service in France. In recognition of his heroic service during a conflict by the American Expeditionary Forces, France made him a member of the Legion of Honor, and his service was noted by General John J. Pershing in his war memoir.

Graduated from Harvard in 1905, Williams spent the next fifteen years working for Williams & Peters, the firm of wholesale coal merchants co-founded by his father in the 1880s. Although *Brookrace* was Williams's primary residence, he also maintained a New York City home on Park Avenue. An avid horse-racing fan, Col. Williams owned the Mendham Stables at Belmont Park, where he kept a number of thoroughbreds. He was a member of many prominent clubs and spent much of his free time hunting and playing golf and polo. In 1905 Col. Williams married Julia Lorillard Edgar, who bore him two daughters and a son.

The *Brookrace* manor house was designed by Ernest Flagg, the Beaux-Arts trained architect whose notable commissions included the Charles Scribner's Sons bookstore on Fifth Avenue in New York and the Singer Building, since demolished, in lower Manhattan, once the world's tallest building. *Brookrace* was noted for its unique architectural style—a combination of Colonial Revival and French Eclectic. In the ballroom stood a magnificent stone fireplace that came from a sixteenth-century French castle. Col. Williams purchased the piece from New York's Princeton Club, which at the time occupied the former Gramercy Park residence of architect Stanford White of the firm McKim, Mead & White. White had brought the fireplace to this country from France and had it installed in his home. At a reported cost of $30,000, Col. Williams had the fireplace dismantled stone by stone and reconstructed at *Brookrace*, where it remains.

Col. Williams, who suffered a nervous breakdown, lived in relatively poor health for many years and died in 1931 at the age of forty-seven. The following year, Mrs. Jacob Schiff bought the estate and donated it to the Boy Scouts of America in memory of her son, Mortimer L. Schiff, a founder of the organization and its president when he died.

In 1933 the Boy Scouts built a thirteen-acre lake on the property. Named Lake Therese in honor of Mrs. Schiff, the lake was created by building a dam across McVickers Brook at the site of a small millpond. It was the millrace along this waterway that had inspired Col. Williams to call his estate *Brookrace*. In the late 1700s the pond fed a gristmill that was used to help supply food to General Washington's army encamped at nearby Jockey Hollow.

The Schiff Reservation served as a national training and education center for Boy Scouts until 1979 when it was purchased by a real estate subsidiary of AT&T. After a long period of often fractious negotiations among the local planning board, private developers, local residents, and environmental groups, the property was subdivided. A private residential community called Brookrace was developed, while three hundred acres were set aside as protected lands under the auspices of the Schiff Natural Lands Trust, which maintains the property and operates walking trails and educational programs there. The old *Brookrace* mansion is privately owned and has been carefully restored in recent years.

GREYSTOCK

Nestled in the hills of Mendham, this two-story brick country manor evokes a sense of immutability, yet it has changed names and owners more than most estates in the area. Its aura of strength and stability apparently appealed to one of its most colorful, if elusive, inhabitants, Albert M. Barnes (1876–1952), a native of Montclair, New Jersey.

Barnes purchased the eighty-acre estate in 1928 from Katharine Minturn LeRoy, who, along with her then-husband, Edward, commissioned the New York architectural firm Lord & Hewlett to design the home in 1915. A local news article in *The Jerseyman,* predating the construction, described plans for "a large summer home with the usual barns, garage, and cottages for employees transforming the tract from farmland to modern summer home." The LeRoys called their idyll *Rockwood.*

A partner in the Wall Street brokerage firm Dillon, Read & Company, Albert Barnes gained some publicity in

1925 for the firm's role in the purchase of Dodge Brothers Motor Car Company. In what was billed as the largest cash transaction in business history to that time, financier Clarence Dillon wrote a single check for $146 million in New York while Barnes was stationed in Detroit to accept title to the company. The deal trumped rival financier J. P. Morgan who sought to acquire the company for General Motors.

A collector of rare cars, Barnes stored several of his prized possessions in his six-car garage, among them a custom-made Locomobile—the most expensive car in the United States in 1923—a 1932 Rolls-Royce, and a Minerva Club coupe. Every car in his stock, which included a 1937 Lincoln Zephyr and a 1941 Lincoln Continental, was painted gray with a black stripe, with Barnes's monogram on the door. He named his estate *Greystock,* perhaps an allusion to his car collection.

An active sportsman, Barnes spent much of his free time hunting and fishing. He was a lifelong bachelor and shared his home with his brother, Frank, and a friend, Dayton K. Price. Ohio-based historian David W. Schultz, who eventually purchased Barnes's Locomobile, traveled to New Jersey in the early 1990s to collect information about the car's original owner, who was a recluse. Schultz discovered much about Barnes's cars, but little about the man himself, except that he was distinctive looking, wore tweed knickers, and hired only Chinese or Filipino servants. Schultz reflected: "For a man of Barnes's wealth, hardly anything remains today of Barnes the man."

Barnes died in 1952 at the age of seventy-six. The estate was sold the following year and has changed hands more than half a dozen times since.

New York architects Lord & Hewlett designed the house—originally named Rockwood—in 1915 for Katharine and Edward LeRoy. Albert M. Barnes acquired the property in 1928 and renamed it Greystock.

FRANKLIN FARMS

FRANKLIN FARMS, a once-sprawling estate that covered more than 400 acres, has served as the residence of a New Jersey governor and a prominent inventor, as well as the campus of a private school. The present estate's rich and eclectic history dates to 1909 when Franklin Murphy (1846–1920), New Jersey's thirty-fifth governor, began to acquire land and hired architect H. Van Buren Magonigle to design the Colonial Revival mansion, which was built of locally quarried fieldstone. The formal gardens, including a sunken one, that graced the property were created by the Olmsted Brothers firm of landscape architects. This famous firm also worked with the Essex County Park Commission, on which Murphy served, in establishing one of the country's earliest county park systems.

Murphy's residence was built on the site of what had been, since the mid-1800s, one of Morris County's largest and most lavish homes, known as *Myrtle Hill* and, later, *Oliver Hall*. This Greek Revival structure was designed by Major Aaron Hudson for Joseph Watkins, stepson of a local Presbyterian minister, who had squandered his sizable inheritance, reportedly lighting his cigars using dollar bills. The home subsequently served as an elegant boarding house operated by Francis Oliver, who was later the proprietor of another boarding house in Bernardsville that evolved into the large resort hotel known as the Somerset Inn.

Franklin Farms was heralded for its fine design and sensitivity to the surrounding landscape. The house had a simple and unpretentious layout. There were large open terraces on the northern and southern sides, allowing in much light. The buildings on the estate were connected with a well-considered road plan. Attractive fencing and shrubbery ensured that the gardener's cottage, piggeries, poultry houses, laundry, and farm buildings were out of sight of the main house yet nearby. Visitors to the house never forgot the floor-to-ceiling pipe organ that Murphy installed after teaching himself to play the instrument late in life.

A love of business, politics, and public service inspired the life of Franklin Murphy, who was raised in Newark. As a child, Murphy attended Newark Academy but left in 1862, at the age of sixteen, to fight in the Civil War. For the next three years, he was on active duty, fighting in

This aerial image of Franklin Farms was taken between 1928 and 1942. The main house is in the upper middle.

many battles including Antietam, Chancellorsville, Gettysburg, Chattanooga, and Lookout Mountain. In some battles, he served under General Sherman. By the end of the war, Murphy had become a first lieutenant. In 1865, using money from his father, a shoe manufacturer, Murphy founded a varnish-manufacturing business in Newark, which eventually expanded into other cities between Boston and Chicago. Murphy Varnish Company gained a national presence, and its president earned national exposure.

Although keenly involved in running his business, Murphy continued to pursue his interest in public service and remained active in Republican politics. By 1886 he had risen to the role of president of the Newark Board of Aldermen, where he was instrumental in running electricity for street lighting and improving the city's parks. He then served in the New Jersey Assembly and in 1892 became chairman of the Republican State Committee. Nine years later, Murphy received the Republican nomination for gov-

ernor and readily defeated his opponent, Mayor James M. Seymour of Newark, to become governor in 1902.

Murphy was the first businessman in New Jersey to serve as governor, and he drew on his business savvy to run the state. During his term in office, Murphy enacted the state's first primary-election law and helped pass strict child-labor laws, a workshop-ventilation law, and a tenement-house law. He also shook up the old political guard by calling attention to absenteeism among state officials and abolishing the fee system in state and county offices. He also urged officials to build a permanent governor's residence in Trenton. Murphy introduced an audit system for state expenditures and mandated banks to pay interest on state deposits. Throughout his life, Murphy was well liked for his courtesy and good humor. He married Janet Colwell of Newark, and they had two children.

After Murphy's death in 1920, his Mendham estate was sold and eventually became the home of George

Constant Louis Washington (1871–1946), the man credited with developing the process to mass-produce instant coffee. An Englishman by birth, Washington graduated from the University of Bonn in Germany and later invented, patented, and manufactured a petroleum incandescent lamp. He traveled to the United States in 1896 to establish a factory for his kerosene lamp, but lost ownership to unscrupulous promoters and moved to Guatemala. While sipping a cup of coffee on the veranda of his plantation in the mountains, Washington noticed a drop of coffee running down the spout of the pot. It dried into a powder that retained its coffee flavor. From that, he developed his idea for the production of soluble coffee—the first instant coffee—and in 1910 founded the G. Washington Coffee Refining Company in New York.

In 1926 Washington moved his manufacturing facility to Morris Plains and purchased *Franklin Farms* two years later. While in residence, Washington actively farmed the land. He also collected rare birds and animals, including llamas and a zebra, and was an avid photographer who also made his own cameras. Washington sold *Franklin Farms* in 1942 and the following year sold his business to American Home Products Corporation. The estate was eventually subdivided. During the 1970s the mansion and twenty-three acres served as Chartwell Manor, a private school.

Front façade.

Garden designed by Olmsted Brothers.

Architect H. Van Buren Magonigle designed the main residence and the principal outbuildings at Franklin Farms, including the stable.

FAR HILLS

Original clubhouse of the Somerset Hills Country Club, above Ravine Lake.

KNOLLCREST

IT IS FITTING THAT *Knollcrest* in Far Hills was built in the uniquely American Shingle style of architecture, because it was home to a quintessential American success story. Almost entirely self-educated, John Forrest Dillon (1831–1914) is remembered as one of the pre-eminent lawyers and scholars of his time. He was a renowned expert in municipal law, serving as a law professor and as president of the American Bar Association.

Dillon was born in the upstate New York town of Northampton on Christmas Day, 1831, to Thomas Dillon, a farmer of Irish immigrant ancestry, and his wife, Rosannah Forrest. When he was seven years old, Dillon moved with his parents to Davenport in the Iowa Territory, where he lived for forty-two years. The Dillons joined about 500 other pioneers to settle the town, with Thomas Dillon becoming a hotelkeeper.

John Forrest Dillon began studying medicine at seventeen and was in the first graduating class of the Rock Island Medical School. He decided against a career in medicine, however, telling a friend: "I have made a great mistake. I cannot practice medicine in this country without being able to ride a horse, and this I am utterly unable to do. I might as well admit my mistake, and turn my mind to something else." He decided to study law, which

John Forrest Dillon.

he did on his own. He was admitted to the bar of Scott County, Iowa, in 1852, and within a year was named county prosecutor. In 1868, at thirty-six, he was appointed chief justice of the Supreme Court of Iowa, after having served as an associate justice on that court and as a judge of Iowa's Seventh Judicial District Court. The following year, President Ulysses S. Grant appointed him to the United States Court of Appeals for the Eighth Circuit.

In 1879, at forty-eight, after ten years of distinguished service as a federal judge, Dillon resigned from the bench to accept a professorship at the law school of Columbia University in New York City. After three years, he resigned to become general counsel for the Union Pacific Railroad, of which his uncle, Sidney Dillon, was president. He worked closely with the railroad's owner, who was one of the most dynamic and controversial businessmen of that era, Jay Gould. Dillon later became counsel for the Missouri Pacific and the Texas Pacific railroads and eventually for the whole Gould railroad system, rising to became Gould's chief legal advisor and, ultimately, the executor of his estate.

After Gould's death in 1892, Dillon shifted his focus from the corporate to the financial sector, becoming one of the country's top bond counselors. As his reputation grew and the scope of his practice expanded, he helped New York City become the capital of the public finance industry. Dillon played a pivotal role as a member of the Greater New York Commission in 1896–97. His input as a commissioner and member of the all-important drafting committee resulted in a new charter that, effective January 1, 1898, consolidated all of the territory that now makes up the boroughs of Manhattan, the Bronx, Brooklyn, Queens, and Staten Island and formed the present City of New York.

In 1891 Dillon was elected president of the American Bar Association and was chosen to be the Storrs Lecturer at Yale University Law School. He published seminal legal works, including *The Laws and Jurisprudence of England and America*, *Removal of Causes from State to the Federal Courts*, and *The Inns of Court and Westminster Hall*. One of his proudest achievements, first published in 1872, was *Commentaries on the Law of Municipal Corporations*, which had five editions. It is

Knollcrest was built in the mid-1890s. Anna Margery Price Dillon, who had a flair for architectural design, was a primary influence in the planning of the house and grounds.

View of Knollcrest *from* Overleigh, *the estate of John F. Dillon's son, John Milton Dillon.*

his most famous work of legal scholarship, widely considered a legal classic.

In the early 1890s Dillon and his wife of forty years, Anna Margery Price—the eldest child of Hiram Price, a one-time commissioner of the Bureau of Indian Affairs—decided to build a country home. From all reports, Dillon enjoyed close family ties at home. He and his wife had six children, two of whom died in infancy. Joseph Hodges Choate, a prominent New York attorney and close friend, said of Dillon's personal life: "He was not a club man, nor a frequenter of public gatherings, and the time at his command, which was not absorbed by the stern grasp of his profession, was devoted to the most delightful domestic life."

Dillon built *Knollcrest* on fifty acres in Far Hills, which he purchased, in 1894, from his friend Evander H. Schley, a New York land speculator who discovered the beauty of the Somerset Hills in the early 1880s. While the Schleys were the first to create a large estate in Far Hills, the Dillons were not far behind.

Dillon's wife, Anna, had a flair for architectural design and spent the summer of 1894 designing and planning

both the house and grounds of *Knollcrest*. After ground was broken in the fall, Mrs. Dillon spent a great deal of time overseeing every detail of what became a working farm. Suffering from a heart condition, she planned *Knollcrest* from her bed.

Modeled on the Shingle style of estates and resorts along the New England coastline, the rambling three-story residence had turrets, stone accents, open porches, and dormer windows. Dillon gradually added more land to his estate along Mine Brook Road until it made up 250 acres. He and several neighbors along what is now Route 202 planted the maple trees that still line the road between Far Hills and Bernardsville. At about the same time that *Knollcrest* was being established, the Dillons' son John Milton Dillon built his own estate, *Overleigh*, across the road.

John F. Dillon's world was tragically altered in 1898 when his wife and their daughter, Anna Dillon Oliver, were lost at sea when the French steamship, the *Bourgogne,* collided with another ship. The two women were en route to a sanitarium in Carlsbad, Germany, seeking a cure for Mrs. Dillon's poor health. At the time of the accident,

Dillon was convalescing at *Knollcrest* with a broken leg. He was devastated by the news. Three weeks after the shipwreck, the captain of a steamship docking at Philadelphia said he had seen hundreds of the 550 victims floating in the Atlantic Ocean. Upon hearing this, Dillon chartered a steamer and sent a party out on a fruitless ten-day search for the bodies of his wife and daughter. Dillon was devoted to his wife's memory and found solace in preparing the story of her life in a memoir he published for her relatives and friends.

John Forrest Dillon remained active throughout his brief retirement years, many of which were spent in Far Hills at

Knollcrest. He died at eighty-three, survived by only one child, his son Hiram P. Dillon, a lawyer in Topeka, Kansas. Dillon's friend Joseph Choate compared him to Abraham Lincoln: "Like Lincoln, he had the indomitable will to succeed, great power of concentration, an insatiable thirst for knowledge, and an intense love of reading."

G. Hermann Kinnicutt, of the Wall Street brokerage firm Kissel, Kinnicutt & Company, purchased *Knollcrest* in 1919, five years after Judge Dillon's death. Kinnicutt subsequently razed the house to build a more modern and fireproof residence. The result was *Mayfields*, an estate he named for his wife, May.

OVERLEIGH

Attorney John Milton Dillon (1868–1911) wanted to build an estate similar to those he had seen in Europe, a dream he fulfilled in his treasured *Overleigh*. Built as a Far Hills summer home for his family, *Overleigh* was an eye-catching American hybrid of French, English, and Italian styles. The mansion had forty-five rooms and covered nearly an acre.

John M. Dillon was born in Davenport, Iowa, the youngest of the six children of Judge John Forrest Dillon and Anna Price Dillon. John received his law degree from Columbia Law School, eventually joining his father's law firm, Dillon, Thomson & Clay, specializing in municipal bonds. In 1891 he married Lucy Sands Downing, with whom he had three children, Madeline Lucy, Milton Sands, and Dorothy Downing.

In 1894 Dillon acquired a nine-room farmhouse and 158 acres from the Schley family. His tract of land was across the road from his father's estate, *Knollcrest*. Over the next ten years, three new wings and an expanded central portion were added to the modest home. Dillon also built cottages, a carriage house, and several farm buildings. He increased his landholdings, eventually acquiring about 225 acres, a significant portion of which his father conveyed to him. The charming wording in the deed accompanying the father-to-son transaction is unusual: "... in consideration of love and affection and the sum of one dollar...."

Dillon's love of horticulture led to his creating an English-style parkland with acres of lawns, rose gardens, shrubbery, and a large variety of specimen trees. A farm and orchard complex at *Overleigh* provided food for the Dillon family and the estate's workers. A two-acre fruit and vegetable garden and chickens, geese, cows, horses, pigs, and beehives contributed to the estate's self-sufficiency.

With elaborate mantelpieces, Flemish quartered-oak woodwork, leaded stained-glass windows, and walls covered in silk brocade, *Overleigh* was designed with great detail. One of the most majestic rooms was the library, fitted with San Domingo mahogany and walls of Spanish leather painted in green and red-gold. It was in this room that Dillon penned much of his writings. With his father, Dillon wrote a three-volume biography of Chief Justice John Marshall, published in 1903. He also wrote *Motor*

Three generations of the Dillon family: (left to right) John Milton, Milton Sands, and John Forrest.

This nine-room house formed the core of what became Overleigh. *After acquiring the house and 158 acres in 1894, John M. Dillon added three wings and enlarged the central portion of the house. It eventually contained forty-five rooms and covered nearly an acre.*

Days in England—a description of an English tour, illustrated by many of his own photographs and pen-and-ink drawings—and a short biography of Edgar Allan Poe, published in 1911. Outside his professional life, Dillon's passion, apart from horticulture, was photography, at which he was accomplished. He took numerous photographs of *Overleigh*, a selection of which are held at the Smithsonian Institution.

Dillon was only forty-two at the time of his death. His wife, Lucy, continued to spend part of her time at the Far Hills estate. The Dillons' son, Milton, an attorney like his father and grandfather, later lived there full-time with his family until his death in 1939, after which the estate was partitioned into two equal tracts shared by his wife, Vera M. Cushman Dillon, and the children of his deceased sister, Dorothy Dillon Page. With the country on the verge of war, and the Depression still taking its toll, farming operations at *Overleigh* ceased, the grounds deteriorated, and the house fell into disrepair.

Although John M. Dillon added to his modest house in the years following 1895 to create a luxurious estate, more than fifty years later his grandson Milton S. Dillon Jr. scaled it down in keeping with the demands and styles of his time. In 1951 Milton tore down the billiard-room wing, the library wing, and the servants' wing. The resulting structure was graceless and out-of-proportion. In the words of one family member, "What was left was a four-and-a-half-story architectural monstrosity."

Since then, thirty-four acres of the property have been acquired by New Jersey's Green Acres program, while the main house has been meticulously renovated to return it to its 1906 condition. With the help of John M. Dillon's photographs of his beloved *Overleigh*, an architect was able to rebuild two of the three wings torn down by Milton Dillon. The 1998 reconstruction also restored many of the estate's plantings. The main house and its surrounding ten acres now look much as they did in the early 1900s.

FROH HEIM

NOT MANY MEN can claim the distinction of having built a town, but Grant Barney Schley (1845–1917) placed himself among the elite few during the late 1800s when he almost single-handedly fashioned the village of Far Hills. Schley's *Froh Heim* estate—now known as *Moorland Farms*—stood at the center of his vast holdings.

Through hard work and a gift for mathematics, Grant Schley rose from humble circumstances to be a wealthy banker and broker. Born near Syracuse, New York, he stopped school at the age of sixteen and went to work as a shipping clerk for Wells, Butterfield & Company. When the company was taken over by the American Express Company, Schley was transferred to New York City. Demonstrating a sharp mathematical aptitude, Schley was rapidly promoted, later joining First National Bank of New York where he ran the bank's foreign-exchange department. In 1879 he married Elizabeth Baker, the sister of George Fisher Baker, a director of American Express and president of First National. In 1881 Schley left the bank and formed the brokerage house of Moore & Schley, which became one of the largest in Wall Street. Schley went on to become president of a number of corporations, amassing a sizable fortune along the way.

Although Grant Schley turned out to be the most influential member of his family, he was not the first to "discover" the Somerset Hills, then a community of small farms. It was his brother, Evander H. Schley (1838–1907), a land speculator, who first visited the area from New York in the early 1880s. Evander, a bachelor, bought hundreds of acres of farmland in Bedminster and Bernards townships, some of it sight unseen.

In 1887 Grant Schley and his wife came out from New York by horse-drawn carriage to have a look at Evander's farms. Elizabeth is said to have exclaimed over the beautiful view of the "far hills," giving name to a place where there was not yet a village. They liked the area so much that they bought several hundred acres along the North Branch of the Raritan River, including the hills still

The second house to be called Froh Heim *was designed by Peabody, Wilson & Brown and built sometime after 1917, partially on the site of the original house. The house was altered in the 1930s by architect F. Burrall Hoffman Jr.*

The original Froh Heim *residence was built by Grant B. Schley. Begun circa 1888, the house was enlarged many times until it eventually measured nearly one-quarter mile around. It was demolished shortly after Schley's death in 1917.*

known as Schley Mountain. Over the years, Grant and Elizabeth bought additional tracts of farmland, eventually amassing an estate of about 3,000 acres.

On a knoll overlooking the river, the Schleys built *Froh Heim*—German for "happy home"—a rambling, eclectic country house with Japanese accents. Over the years they added to it many times in an almost haphazard way as additional space was required until it eventually measured almost a quarter-mile around. The estate included barns, stables, cottages, a blacksmith's shop, orchards, and a racetrack. The Schleys constructed extensive Japanese gardens with a teahouse and adorned the entire estate with monuments, carved lanterns, torii gateways, and pillars made of stone shipped from the Far East. An elaborate pagoda-like tower with a self-hoisting elevator was built on the highest point of Schley Mountain to afford views as far as New York City. The eighty-five-foot-high structure, then considered one of the finest examples of Japanese architecture in the country, had gargoyle-like figures on the corners of each platform. Schley Tower, as it was known, was painted in red with purple balustrades and gold trim adorned with bells. It was linked to a network of roads and bridle paths connecting scenic vistas and points of interest on the estate. The tower and Japanese gardens were used as background scenes in Mary Pickford's 1915 silent movie *Madame Butterfly*.

Schley was not content merely to be lord of his own manor. With a paternalistic benevolence, he also set out to design and shape a community to fit his ideals. In part through his efforts, the Passaic & Delaware Extension Railroad built an extension line from Bernardsville to Gladstone in 1890. Once the railroad came to Far Hills, it was time for Schley, a strapping redhead who was sometimes mistaken for Theodore Roosevelt, to build a village. A subdivision plan was drawn up for farmland in which Evander Schley had bought an interest, and residential lots were put up for sale. On land set aside for community use, Grant Schley paid for the construction of a firehouse, a social hall, and St. Elizabeth's Church, said to have been named after his wife. He built a school and for years underwrote its operating costs. He had floodplains along the river drained, graded, and seeded to become fairgrounds for agricultural and sporting events. He built stables, barns, and a grandstand at the fairgrounds, and organized an athletic club, an agricultural association, and a brass band that played at parades and social events. An oil portrait of Grant Schley hangs in a prominent place in the meeting room of the Far Hills municipal building, a reminder of the town's dynamic founding father.

Grant Schley died in 1917, and *Froh Heim* was taken down by his son, Evander B. Schley (1883–1952)—known as Van—who was a mining industrialist. A new Spanish-style stone-and-stucco house with a red-tile roof was designed by architects Peabody, Wilson & Brown of New

Stables, shown, and a large two-story recreation building were designed for Evander B. Schley, Grant's son, by A. Musgrave Hyde in the 1930s.

York and built partially on the existing foundation. The library paneling was from Czechoslovakia, and the parquet floor in the living room was from a house in France. In the 1930s alterations to the main house were carried out by architect F. Burrall Hoffman Jr. In 1935 Van erected stables and a two-story recreation building, both designed by New York architect A. Musgrave Hyde. In addition to a glass-roofed tennis court pavilion, the recreation building had bowling alleys, game rooms, a living room, and a Turkish bath. A successful beef operation was run on the farm, with *Froh Heim* boasting one of the finest herds of Angus cattle in the East.

Like its predecessor, the new *Froh Heim* often served as a meeting point for hunts of the Essex Fox Hounds. In 1916 the estate began hosting the annual New Jersey Hunt Cup steeplechase—one of the first to be run in the United States. That event evolved into the Far Hills Race Meeting, the October spectacle that continues to this day, attracting crowds of 45,000 and raising funds for the Somerset Medical Center.

Froh Heim passed out of Schley family ownership in 1954, two years after Van's death. One of the subsequent owners was William Bassett, who renamed the estate *Moorland Farms* after a property his family had owned in nearby Pottersville. The heart of the old *Froh Heim* estate is still known as *Moorland Farms* and is owned by the non-profit group that runs the benefit steeplechase.

An archway outside the original Froh Heim *house of Grant and Elizabeth Schley.*

PENNBROOK

THE IMPOSING STONE-AND-STUCCO residence on the western slope of the Bernardsville mountain, still known as *Pennbrook*, was built as a home for the Clarence Blair Mitchell (1865–1956) family. Mitchell, a lawyer, was the grandson of mining and railroad industrialist John Insley Blair. At the same time *Pennbrook* was being built, the legendary Peapack estate *Blairsden* was under construction for Mitchell's first cousin, Clinton Ledyard Blair.

Mitchell was born in New York City. In 1889, the year he graduated from Princeton University—then known as the College of New Jersey—he married Mildred Matthews, whose father was an English surgeon in South Africa. After attending Columbia Law School and being admitted to the bar, Mitchell began his law career with the firm of Dillon & Swayne, of which John Forrest Dillon of *Knollcrest* in Far Hills was the senior partner. He later joined Choate & Larocque, eventually becoming a partner in the firm, which evolved into Choate, Mitchell, Bayes & Baker.

Mitchell and his wife settled in Westchester, New York, but before long began looking for a quieter place to raise their family. After considering the upper Hudson, upper Westchester County, Long Island, and Tuxedo, they decided on the Somerset Hills. In his memoirs, Mitchell wrote that the area was "healthy and unspoiled country, free from mosquitoes, well watered and wooded."

In 1898 the Mitchells purchased fourteen contiguous tracts of land in what is now Far Hills. The name they gave to their estate, *Pennbrook*, was suggested by a brook on the property that flowed by Penn's Corner, which marked one end of a grant to Sir William Penn. Mitchell took an active part in its design, preparing ground plans for the house and stable and planning the upper entrance and lodge as well as the lower entrance and drive. The gates were copied from a photograph that Mitchell had taken of gates in Algiers. William Russell of the firm Clinton & Russell was the principal architect, and Edward Burnett assisted with the plans for the farm barns. The grounds, gardens, terrace, and upper drive were laid out by landscape architect James Leal Greenleaf, who assisted in the design of *Blairsden's* gardens at about the same time.

The main house at *Pennbrook* was built in the Tudor Revival style with half-timbering, intersecting gables, and pitched-roof dormers. The masonry work was carried out by local construction engineer Frank Tainter, using stone quarried on site, except for the doorways and cornerstones, which were from Snake Hill Quarry in Peapack on Arthur Turnbull's estate. Mitchell hired builders from Westchester—William Henderson and his father—who he described as "master builders of the old school who took great pride in their work." For the woodwork, the Hendersons used old oak stored in their yard for more than a generation. The massive locust posts in the stable each represent a Westchester tree.

The Mitchells moved into *Pennbrook* in 1903 and soon became involved in local life. In addition to raising their son and four daughters, Mildred Mitchell was active in the community. She was a founder of the Visiting Nurse Association of Somerset Hills, serving as its president for more than ten years, the first president of the board of education in Far Hills, head of the Somerset County Health Association, and president of the Women's State Republican Club of New Jersey.

Clarence Mitchell, a keen sportsman and a founding member of the Somerset Hills Country Club, claimed to be one of the first to play golf in America, although he admitted to being temperamentally unsuited to the game. Horses were his real passion, and throughout his life he rode and hunted, often traveling to Geneseo in upstate New York to buy horses and hunt. While at Princeton, he often rode the thirty miles to his father's home at Lakewood, New Jersey. Mitchell was one of the founders of the Essex Fox Hounds when the pack was taken over from Charles Pfizer in 1913. Mitchell twice hosted a gymkhana at *Pennbrook*. He also enjoyed driving and had a collection of carriages, with wheels painted yellow to conform with the family livery of black and primrose yellow.

The Mitchells traveled extensively throughout Europe for business and pleasure and established many friendships

Clarence Blair Mitchell's friend, architect William Russell of the New York firm of Clinton & Russell, designed Pennbrook, although Mitchell laid out the ground plan. Landscape architect James Leal Greenleaf, who worked at Blairsden, Upton Pyne, and Wendover, laid out the gardens, terrace, and upper drives. The Mitchells moved into the house in November 1903.

abroad. The guest book at *Pennbrook* contains almost 2,000 names of visitors from all over the world. They filled their house with antiques and artifacts acquired on their trips, among them a 200-year-old oak chest and tapestry from Dinan, France; an English oak dresser dating from the reign of Charles II; an Arab bridal chest from Algiers; and a mahogany armchair that George Washington was said to have sat on. In the library, there were rare pamphlets, maps, and sets of books, many of them from the collection of Mitchell's paternal ancestors in South Carolina. There was a set of Leicestershire hunting prints from Paris and one of the most complete collections of prints of Charleston to be found anywhere. There were two eighteenth-century silver tea caddies from the Washington family in England, as well as trays and bowls and plates and cups from Europe, Africa, and Asia.

Mitchell was a prolific writer, author of the *History of the Ivy Club, Thoughts on Political Democracy, Some Reminiscences,* and the *Mitchell Record*. While at Princeton, he wrote the words of "The Orange and the Black," scribbled on a midnight train from Philadelphia. For his children and grandchildren, he wrote a short instruction manual, *The A B C of Riding to Hounds,* and an ode to the home he loved, *On Pennbrook Hill.*

After Mitchell died in 1956, in his ninety-first year, his wife moved to a cottage on the estate. *Pennbrook* was sold by the Mitchell family in the 1960s after Mildred's death. There have since been only two principal owners, both of whom retained not only the estate's original name, but also its architectural integrity.

Clarence Mitchell designed the estate's upper entrance and lodge. The gates were copied from a photograph he took of gates in Algiers.

TEVIOT FARM

TEVIOT FARM, built in 1914, was originally the home of Arthur Turnbull (1865–1939), a governor of the New York Stock Exchange, and his wife, Alice W. Post, the only daughter of architect George B. Post. Located at the foot of the Bernardsville mountain overlooking the North Branch of the Raritan River, the farm offered not only easy access to water and lush grazing pastures for the animals, but also a charming setting for the main residence. The name the Turnbulls chose for their property derives from the Teviot River in Scotland, the ancestral land of the family. Over a thirty-year period, beginning at the end of the 1890s, the Turnbulls acquired a substantial estate in the Peapack valley, amounting to more than 700 acres of land.

Arthur Turnbull was born in New York City and attended St. Mark's School and Columbia University, from which he was graduated in 1886 before taking a job with the Delaware & Hudson Railroad. He later joined the United States Mortgage and Trust Company as vice president and treasurer. When it was absorbed by the Chemical Bank & Trust Company, he became a director of the combined firm. In 1902 he was elected a member of the New York Stock Exchange and soon after joined the brokerage firm of Post & Flagg, of which he became a senior partner. From 1915 to 1935 he was a governor of the exchange, for much of that time serving on its law committee, of which he was chairman during the chaotic events of 1929. Turnbull was also a member of the Chicago Board of Trade.

Turnbull married Alice Post in 1907. The couple lived in New York City and initially summered at *Claremont*, the Bernardsville mountain estate of Turnbull's father-in-law. Soon after Post's death in 1913, the stone-and-stucco residence at *Teviot Farm* was completed. George B. Post's sons, James Otis and William Stone, who continued their father's architectural firm after his death, are credited with the design of the house.

Turnbull was active in the community, both in New Jersey and New York. He was a founding board member of the Essex Fox Hounds in Peapack in 1913 and the Somerset Lake and Game Club in Far Hills in 1917. Turnbull served as president of the Union Club, New York's oldest social club, from 1930 to 1938. During his tenure, the

Teviot Farm has extensive frontage along the North Branch of the Raritan River. George B. Post's sons, James Otis and William Stone, who were partners in the family's architectural firm of George B. Post & Sons, are credited with the design of the house, which was completed soon after the senior Post's death in 1913.

club's new premises were built at Sixty-ninth Street and Park Avenue.

Arthur and Alice Turnbull had two children, Arthur Jr. and William. After Turnbull died in 1939, Arthur Jr. moved into the main residence at *Teviot Farm* and lived there until his death in 1985. His brother, William, and William's wife, Elizabeth Thomas Howe, then moved into the house. William, who died in 2002, studied architecture at Yale and at Cranbrook Academy of Art in Michigan under Eliel Saarinen. But his main occupation was managing the family farm. He was a passionate and hard-working land conservationist and made his mark in the area by preserving open space on a substantial portion of his property through the donation of conservation easements. In 1959 Turnbull helped found the Upper Raritan Watershed Association, one of the area's principal conservation organizations.

Behind *Teviot Farm's* main house is a quarry, once known as Snake Hill Quarry, which provided the stone for many of the construction projects in the area, including the Ravine Lake dam, built in 1898–99. Near the quarry is a stonecutter's cottage, built around 1830. It was typical of William Turnbull's commitment to preservation that when the cottage was being stabilized, he went to great lengths to ensure that the repairs were consistent with early-nineteenth-century building methods, refusing to have heating or electricity installed.

One of William Turnbull's four children, William Jr., made his mark in the field of architecture, as his great-grandfather, George B. Post, had before him. William Jr. achieved national recognition for his work on the Sea Ranch condominium complex in Sonoma County on the California coast. The project, completed in the mid-1960s, inspired a new generation of California architecture with its sculptural wooden structures. Turnbull designed many buildings in the United States and overseas, including a winery in the Napa Valley, a library in Mississippi, the American Club in Hong Kong, and his own home in Sonoma County, which he named *Teviot Springs*. Turnbull had a lifelong collaboration with noted architect and teacher, Charles Moore, whom he met while studying at the École des Beaux-Arts. Shortly before Turnbull's death in 1997, he and Moore wrote a book about "the world's profound spaces"—*The Poetics of Gardens*.

Teviot Farm remains in the Turnbull family and continues to be run as a working farm, breeding black Angus cattle.

CRESTLINE

FRANK STONE TAINTER (1862–1941), who built *Crestline* in Far Hills, is responsible for two of the most enduring icons of the golden age of the Somerset Hills: the Ravine Lake dam and the map of *Hamilton Farm*. Born in Morristown to Thomas and Josephine Tainter, Frank Tainter trained and worked as a construction engineer. Early in his career, he was employed as a draftsman for the Metropolitan Telephone & Telegraph Company in New York City. Later, he was associated with the New York-based engineering firm of Parsons, Klapp, Brinckerhoff & Douglas. During World War I, Tainter served as a lieutenant colonel in the Engineering Corps of the United States Army.

Tainter worked on many engineering projects around the country, including Carnegie Lake at Princeton University and Detroit's river tunnel. In the 1930s he served as head of the research and engineering committee of a commission set up to reduce water pollution in New York, New Jersey, and Connecticut. Closer to his home, Tainter was involved in the construction of many of the mansions that were erected in the area around the turn of the twentieth century, including Percy Pyne's *Upton Pyne*, Clarence Blair Mitchell's *Pennbrook*, C. Ledyard Blair's *Blairsden*,

George B. Post Jr.'s *Kenilwood*, and Henry Young's *Brushwood*. But the engineering project for which he is best remembered was the construction in 1898–99 of a dam to create Ravine Lake, which provided bathing and recreation facilities for the newly formed Somerset Hills Country Club. In 1918 the club moved to its present location in Bernardsville and the Somerset Lake & Game Club was formed for swimming, boating, and fishing on the lake. Tainter served on the boards of both clubs.

As the town engineer for virtually all the municipalities in the Somerset Hills, Tainter designed many roads and bridges in the area and drew many of the area's early survey maps, including a 1919 trail map for the newly formed Somerset Hills Bridle Path Association. His most notable achievement in draftsmanship, however, was the 1925 map of James Cox Brady's *Hamilton Farm*. Today treasured by those fortunate enough to own an original, the map not only outlines the boundaries of Brady's 5,000-acre estate encompassing large sections of Somerset, Hunterdon, and Morris counties, but it also identifies the meeting places of the Essex Fox Hounds, bridle paths, property owners, and such lore as the grave of Lenape Indian Chief Paul. The Somerset County engineer at the time, Oscar Smith, did the lettering and sketched the horse, hound, and fox, while Smith's wife and the women of Peapack hand-colored the maps. A second edition of the map was published in 1935.

Tainter married Susan Bayard, a relative of the Stevens family, founders of the world's first college devoted to engineering, the Stevens Institute of Technology, in Hoboken. *Crestline* was built in 1899, the same year that Tainter oversaw construction of the Ravine Lake dam. Perhaps to provide a view of one of his achievements, Tainter located his stone house on the hillside just across the road from the dam. In 1938 fire caused by sparks from the chimney destroyed the house. Firemen laid 1,500 feet of hose from Ravine Lake up the hill to *Crestline* but were unable to contain the blaze. It is believed that portraits of George and Martha Washington by Gilbert Stuart were destroyed in the fire. The house was rebuilt within the original stone walls. Tainter died just three years after the fire. His wife remained in the house until her own death in 1954.

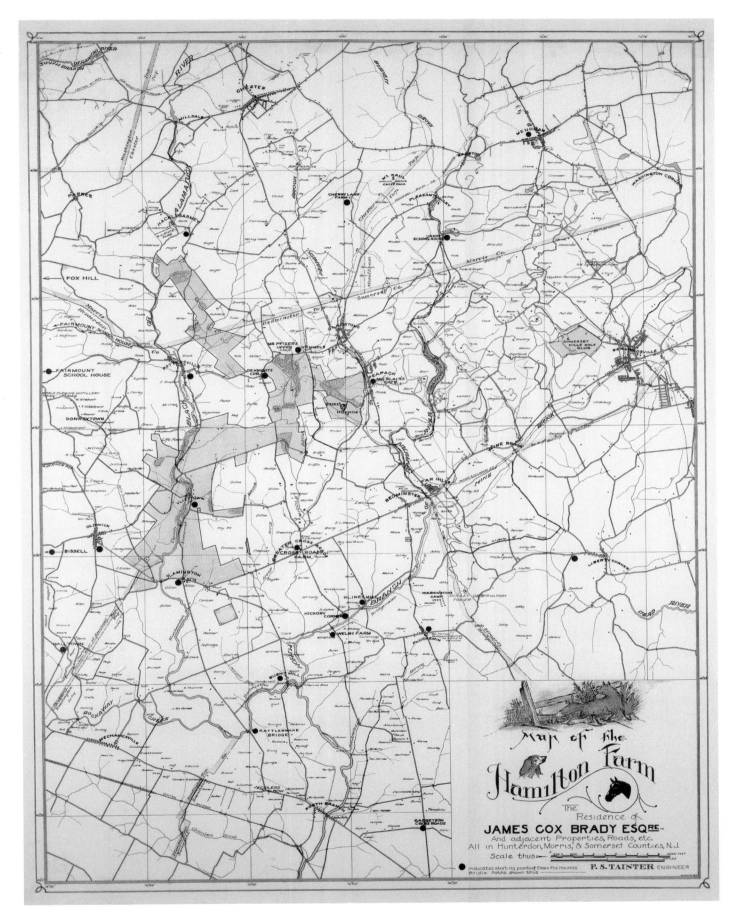

The 1925 map of Hamilton Farm.

PEAPACK-GLADSTONE

C. Ledyard Blair driving his four-in-hand coach, Defiance, out of Blairsden.

BLAIRSDEN

Blairsden was the legendary Peapack estate of financier, sportsman, and banking heir Clinton Ledyard Blair (1867–1949), the descendant of an old, prominent, and wealthy New Jersey family. Ledyard Blair's great-great-grandfather was John Blair, who came to this country from Scotland in the 1730s and fought in the American Revolution. His grandfather, John Insley Blair, made a fortune in the coal- and iron ore-mining and railroad industries. John I. Blair was a longtime trustee and major benefactor of Princeton University and, in 1848, established and endowed Blair Academy, a college preparatory school in Blairstown, New Jersey.

After graduating from Princeton in 1890, Ledyard Blair joined his father, DeWitt Clinton Blair, and his grandfather in forming the New York investment banking firm of Blair & Company. Later, he served on the board of governors of the New York Stock Exchange, as commodore of the New York Yacht Club, and as a trustee and member of many other civic and social organizations in New York and New Jersey. He was also a founder and first president of the Somerset Hills Country Club.

Beginning in 1897, Blair and his wife, Florence Osborne Jennings, purchased several farms in what is Peapack-Gladstone, including a large tract of land from the newly formed Ravine Association, ultimately amassing an estate of some 500 acres where they built their primary and most cherished residence, *Blairsden*. At first, Blair's friends objected, telling him Somerset County was too far from New York City. Undaunted, Blair forged ahead and selected the crown of the highest hill on the property as the home site.

Blair selected the prominent New York architectural firm of Carrère & Hastings to design *Blairsden*, in part because Thomas Hastings, a quintessential gentleman architect of his time, was a family friend. Hastings and his partner, John Merven Carrère, who were among the most influential American architects of their time, were dedicated proponents of the Beaux-Arts style. The firm is best known for its design of the New York Public Library on Fifth Avenue. Among its other notable commissions were the Frick mansion in New York, the Henry Flagler mansion —*Whitehall*—in Palm Beach, and the House and Senate office buildings in Washington, D.C.

The images on this page were taken in 1903 shortly after the house
was completed.

Top: This oblique view shows the elaborate limestone pedimented entrance on
the left and the arched openings of the orangery below the terrace. The original
clubhouse of the Somerset Hills Country Club, located on the opposite hillside
above Ravine Lake, can be seen in the upper right.

Above: This walled garden was located off the dining room. The pergola and
belvedere are on the right.

Above, right: The belvedere, or summer pavilion, which was connected to the
house by a pergola, afforded views over Ravine Lake to distant hills.

Right: The living room looking toward the library at the far end.

A 300-foot-long reflecting pool and nineteenth-century Italian wellhead graced the main entrance to Blairsden. The driveway encircling the pool was lined with busts of the first twelve Roman Caesars and full-grown maple trees that were hauled to the hilltop site by teams of sixteen horses.

This Italian marble satyr is one of four that originally graced the terrace wall overlooking Ravine Lake.

Members of the extended Blair family were among Carrère & Hastings' most important and regular clients. In addition to *Blairsden*, the firm designed Ledyard Blair's residence on Fifth Avenue in New York, across Seventieth Street from the Frick mansion (the Blair house was later demolished to make way for an apartment building); the towered boathouse at the Blairs' Bermuda estate, *Deepdene*; alterations to the family's Trowbridge & Livingston-designed stable and artist's studio at 123 East Sixty-third Street in New York; the Blair & Company office building on Broad Street in New York (demolished); the J. Insley Blair (Ledyard's brother) residence in Tuxedo, New York; the James A. Blair (Ledyard's cousin) estate, *Ontare*, in Oyster Bay Cove, New York; and *Vernon Court*, the Newport estate of Mrs. Richard Gambrill, whose son, Richard Van Nest Gambrill, married Ledyard Blair's daughter, Edith.

The construction of the main house at *Blairsden* was hailed as a marvel of planning and engineering. First, the hill's peak was sliced off and then a miniature inclined railway, complete with a wood-burning engine, was built to haul building materials to the work site. Carrère & Hastings designed a three-story brick and limestone house loosely based on the Louis XIII Chateau style, with a high pitched roof that successfully mimicked the hill on which the house sat.

Designed and constructed between 1898 and 1903— with alterations by Carrère & Hastings made sometime after 1915—*Blairsden* was assembled using the finest available materials, including Indiana and French limestone, face brick, slate for the roof, ornamental copper and bronze, and magnificent interior stone, wood, and plaster finishes. In addition to its elaborate design and decorative elements, the mansion included many state-of-the-art technological and construction features, such as full electrical service, elevators, a steel superstructure, poured-concrete floors from basement to attic, and advanced water supply and ventilation systems.

The gardens and grounds were the vision of Thomas Hastings and landscape architect James Leal Greenleaf. Greenleaf, who taught and practiced civil engineering before turning to landscape architecture, got his first important landscape commission in the late 1890s when, with the Olmsted Brothers firm, he helped transform James B. Duke's vast acreage near Somerville, New Jersey, into a parklike estate. Later, as a member of the National Commission of Fine Arts, Greenleaf was instrumental in the landscape designs for the Lincoln Memorial and Arlington Memorial Bridge in Washington, D.C., and the United States military cemeteries established in Europe after World War I.

At *Blairsden*, Hastings and Greenleaf contrived an elaborate Italianate garden with stone and brick staircases, fountains and mosaic-tile ramps forming a dramatic axial allée running from the terrace down the steep hillside above Ravine Lake. About twenty formally landscaped acres around the house included a rose garden, which is said to have included about 1,400 types of rose bushes, an intimate walled garden behind the main house, tennis courts with an adjacent brick and lattice pavilion, wisteria-crowned arbors overlooking the lake, and extensive water works, including pools, fountains, cascades, and water jets. The *New York Daily Tribune* reported that more than seventy-five full-grown trees with trunks twenty inches in diameter and up to sixty feet tall were moved by wagons pulled by teams of sixteen horses over ten miles of mountain roads and placed along the entrance drive, around the reflecting

pool, and throughout the grounds. Sweeping green lawns, rhododendron, forsythia, magnolia, dogwood, and wisteria adorned the property.

The integration of house and landscape at *Blairsden* has been called one of the finest Beaux-Arts ensembles in the country. A mile-long drive lined with linden trees and a Norman-style stone wall led to the splendid hilltop setting overlooking Ravine Lake, fed by the North Branch of the Raritan River, beyond which were gently rolling hills. A 300-foot-long reflecting pool, flanked by marble busts of the first twelve Roman Caesars and giant sugar maples, led to the richly carved limestone entrance. Housing for the literally dozens of indoor and outdoor staff members was provided among numerous bedrooms on the third floor, in quarters in and near the coach barn, and in cottages on the estate.

The main entrance to the thirty-eight-room house was through two heavy bronze doors constructed with one-inch-thick plate glass and each weighing more than 1,000 pounds. The main cross hall featured a broad, curving limestone double stairway complemented by a sterling silver and bronze chandelier. The main dining room was decorated with elaborate plaster moldings and pilasters, and the ceiling was inset with old French and Italian oil paintings. There were twenty-five fireplaces, all adorned with uniquely detailed mantels. Palatial rooms were ornamented with imported marble, limestone, and tile; brass, sterling silver, and bronze fittings; ornate sconces and chandeliers; intricate plaster and stonework; and carved millwork of walnut, oak, and mahogany. Author and well-known architectural critic Barr Feree gave *Blairsden* pride of place as the subject of the opening chapter in his 1904 book, *American Estates and Gardens*. He described it as "one of

the most elaborate and extensive schemes of its kind ever carried out in America."

By all accounts, the Blairs had many houseguests and frequently hosted parties at *Blairsden*. All four Blair daughters—Marjory, Florence, Edith, and Marise—celebrated their weddings at the Peapack estate, each a major social event. For Marjory's wedding in 1913, a special train brought guests from Hoboken's Lackawanna Terminal to Peapack. When the girls were young, they spent many happy hours in a specially designed playroom with miniature arched doorways and a tiny bathroom. Grand as the house was, having four active children under the roof lent an air of informality. After horseback riding, the Blair girls and their friends were allowed to lounge in the living room, still dressed in their muddy gear. Their mother, Florence, was full of fun and arranged costume, birthday, and Fourth of July parties, Easter egg hunts, and Christmas plays. Christmas parties included a jolly Santa Claus emerging from one of the large chimneys to delight the children. In 1915 the house and gardens served as the backdrop for the silent movie, *Poor Little Peppina*, starring Mary Pickford.

Like many of the great country estates of the period, *Blairsden* was built for the sporting life, with miles of horse trails and coaching roads, a boathouse, a horse track, and a trap shoot with its own shooting lodge. To extend the season, the tennis courts were covered with boards and canvas in the winter months and the tennis pavilion had a fireplace to warm the players. The basement of the house held a squash court, Turkish baths, and what was known as the "plunge," a deep indoor pool with no shallow end.

In *The Architecture of Carrère and Hastings*, a Columbia University dissertation by Curtis Channing Blake, the

Opposite: *The estate's entrance gates were designed by Carrère & Hastings. (Left) The original main entrance gate was located below Ravine Lake dam. It was constructed circa 1902 and featured a ram's-head fountain on a curved limestone wall. (right) The Main Street entrance, which included a series of pools and fountains and a brick loggia along the driveway beyond the gate, was built circa 1909–10.*

Left: *C. Ledyard Blair and two of his four daughters.*

Below: *A Blair wedding on the terrace overlooking Ravine Lake.*

Cross hall looking from the main entrance vestibule; bronze statue of Joan of Arc on pedestal.

author described *Blairsden* as "the finest Edwardian country house in America."

The house along with its extensive gardens, pools, lake, farm buildings and forests, stands as the apotheosis of the year round American country residence. It is hard to imagine a more idyllic and graceful situation for the playing out of Edwardian country life. The architects have provided all the appurtenances for a wealthy gentleman's rural regimen, which included family life, large scale social entertaining, the raising of horses and livestock, the care of woodlands and streams, and the general enjoyment of the dramatic natural setting.

Ledyard Blair lived at *Blairsden* for forty-seven years. His first wife, Florence, died in New York City in 1931 after a long illness. Five years later he married Harriet S. Browne Tailer. After Blair's death in 1949, the property was broken up and sold. In 1950 the contents of the house were sold at a public auction at *Blairsden* handled by Parke-Bernet

Galleries Inc. The same year, the house and fifty surrounding acres were sold for $65,000 to an order of Catholic nuns, the Sisters of St. John the Baptist, who renamed it St. Joseph's Villa and operated it as a retreat for women until the 1990s. The order sold the propery in 2002.

Today, *Blairsden* is a tangible reminder of an era when lavish estates combined the finest elements of style, design, detail, and luxury. Architecturally, the house is much the same as when the Blair family lived there. Although *Blairsden* retains just thirty acres, much of the structural elements of the original landscape architecture remain, as do some of the original plantings. Incredibly, the area surrounding *Blairsden* and the magnificent views of Ravine Lake and the Raritan River watershed remain much as they were a century ago. Fortunately, that is because much of the estate's original acreage has remained in large, undeveloped tracts, some owned by Blair family descendants,

The dining room was altered and enlarged for the Blairs by Carrère & Hastings sometime after 1915.

HILLANDALE

O F PEAPACK-GLADSTONE'S turn-of-the-century grand estates, *Hillandale* undoubtedly has the saddest and most tragic history. The story begins with a merchant born in Germany by the name of George Rudolf Mosle (1865–1941) whose family firm, Mosle Brothers, was involved in shipping and the sugar trade. In 1891 Mosle married Katherine Kunhardt, the sister of Henry Kunhardt who built *Blythewood* on the Bernardsville mountain at the end of the nineteenth century. Like the Mosles, the German-born Kunhardt family was engaged in the shipping industry and the sugar trade.

Beginning in late 1899, the Mosles acquired 650 acres in what is Peapack-Gladstone and Mendham Township. Mosle commissioned architect Grosvenor Atterbury—who had received his education at Columbia University and the École des Beaux-Arts in Paris and had received his early training at the firm of McKim, Mead & White—to design his house on the highest hilltop on the estate. The result was a large, but gracefully proportioned, fifty-room mansion of brick and stone. The interior of the home was decorated by "the misses Whittredge and Barrows," who were also decorating the home of John D. Rockefeller Jr. Landscaped gardens were planned around the house, and numerous farm and outbuildings were built, including dairy barns, in accordance with Mosle's ambition to create a working farm. Maple trees, some of which remain, lined the long and winding entrance road that led to the house from Gladstone. Although the firm of McKim, Mead & White is said to have designed the stone-and-steel seven-car garage and staff apartment building on the estate, no evidence of this has been found, and the story may well be a reference to Atterbury who had worked at the firm.

George and Katherine Mosle lived at *Hillandale*, after its completion in 1906, for about thirteen years, raising two sons and two daughters. During World War I, Mosle suffered significant financial losses when his ships were sunk by German submarines. Mosle's grandson and namesake has recalled that Mosle Brothers had invested heavily in the Cuban sugar trade and that, because ships were being sunk and the firm could not transport the sugar cane to the United States, the crop rotted on the docks, thereby contributing to the financial ruin of the family firm. After the war, Mosle filed one of the largest individual war claims against Germany, but it is doubtful he recovered much, if anything, on the claim due to delays inherent in the claims process and Germany's economic ruin after the war. The Mosles were forced to put *Hillandale* on the market. They moved out of the large main residence and into a small wood-frame house on the property. In 1919 *Hillandale* was sold and the family moved to California, first to a ranch in Ojai and later to Santa Barbara.

The estate was purchased at auction by a New York paper manufacturing firm, Wilkinson Brothers & Company, for $110,000. Five years later, in 1924, it was sold to William B. Wetmore and then repurchased by Wilkinson two years after that in a foreclosure sale. *Hillandale* was sold again, in 1926, to a Roman Catholic order, the Sisters of St. John the Baptist. The Sisters founded an orphanage on the estate, which they named Villa O'Connor after Bishop O'Connor of the Newark Diocese. The main house was converted to accommodate the nuns and girls, and the stables were refurbished to serve as the boys' dormitory. On a cold winter's night in 1927, a fire broke out in the boys' dormitory. Despite the heroic efforts of the nuns—they fought their way into the fire to pull out seventy-six boys, and one nun was said to have run to Gladstone to raise the alarm—three boys perished and two nuns were injured. The fire was all the more tragic because Mosle, a founder of the Peapack-Gladstone Fire Department, tried to ensure that the buildings at *Hillandale* were fireproof.

The Sisters raised sufficient funds to rebuild the boys' dormitory, which was completed in 1934. A few years later, Villa O'Connor closed its doors, and the Sisters founded a private school that they called St. John's School. Soon after, a summer camp for city children, Camp St. John, was established, for which cabins and a swimming pool were built.

As the school grew, two large brick-and-stone wings were added to the main building, and a chapel and additional classroom space were built. In 1949 the school was expanded to include high school grades, and its name was changed to Mount St. John Academy. Today, the nuns lease part of the estate to Montgomery Academy, a private day school for children with disabilities.

*Completed in 1906, Hillandale was designed for George and Katherine
Kunhardt Mosle by Grosvenor Atterbury, who also designed the house known
as Green Gables and Baricross in Bernardsville.*

NATIRAR

IN MARCH 2003, the 500-acre *Natirar* estate began a new phase of its long and storied history when it was acquired by Somerset County from the estate of His Majesty Hassan II, the late King of Morocco. The property, which sprawls across parts of Peapack-Gladstone, Far Hills, and Bedminster, lies above the confluence of the North Branch of the Raritan River and the Peapack Brook. Some of the region's earliest European settlement—dating to the early 1740s—occurred on what is now the estate.

For the past century, however, the property has been primarily associated with the Ladd family, who created the present estate and called it *Natirar*—Raritan spelled backwards. Walter Graeme Ladd (1857–1933) and his wife, Catherine Everit Macy Ladd (1863–1945), began to acquire land in the area in 1905, purchasing from Zachariah Belcher, William Stone Post, and Evander H. Schley, among others. Eventually the Ladds created one of the largest estates in the area, encompassing nearly 1,000 acres, through which the North Branch of the Raritan River meanders for two miles.

The Ladds' 30,000-square-foot Tudor-style mansion was completed in 1912, after about two years of construction. Built of brick with limestone trim and a slate roof, it featured extensive oak paneling, teak floors, and molded plaster ceilings. The main house, several of the principal outbuildings, and the overall layout of the estate were principally designed by Guy Lowell, a Boston-born architect and landscape architect who was from a prominent New England family whose relatives included the poets James Russell Lowell and Amy Lowell and Harvard University president A. Lawrence Lowell. In 1907 Guy Lowell had designed the Ladds' summer residence in Bar Harbor, Maine—*Eegonos,* a backwards spelling of Sonogee Point, where the house was located.

Lowell was a skilled architect whose work was broad in scope, comprising large public, academic, and commercial buildings, as well as many distinctive residences, country

The 30,000-square-foot residence at Natirar was designed by Boston architect Guy Lowell and completed in 1912.

Natirar's *hilltop location affords expansive views extending south toward Somerville, the Sourland Mountains, and Princeton. The flat-roofed conservatory on the south terrace was added circa 1949 when the house was converted to convalescent home use. The wing on the left was originally a teahouse for Mrs. Ladd.*

This photograph of the north façade was taken in 1912 as construction was nearing completion.

estates, and formal gardens. He is perhaps most famous for his design of two public buildings, the Boston Museum of Fine Arts, the first section of which was completed in 1909, and the hexagonal New York County Courthouse on Foley Square in Manhattan, built between 1913 and 1927. His residential work in New York and New England comprised the bulk of his practice. Other than *Natirar*, Lowell's only known commission in New Jersey, however, was the circa-1905 Harden L. Crawford residence in Sea Bright.

Lowell was assisted in the design of *Natirar* by Henry Janeway Hardenbergh, a New Brunswick-born architect who practiced in New York and is most famous for his designs there of the luxury apartment building known as the Dakota on Central Park West and the Plaza Hotel. In the 1880s Hardenbergh designed his own summer cottage, *Renemede,* on the Bernardsville mountain.

Catherine Everit Macy—known as Kate—was born in New York, the second of three children of Josiah Macy Jr. and Caroline Louise Everit Macy. Kate was a descendant of the original settlers of Salisbury, Massachusetts, Thomas and Sarah Macy, who came to America about 1635 from the parish of Chilmark near Salisbury, England. In 1659 Thomas Macy and his family moved to Nantucket Island where he worked in the whaling industry. Thomas prospered in the thriving business and was one of several men who later purchased the island. The Thomas Macy house still stands in Nantucket town.

In the early-nineteenth century, Kate Macy's great-grandfather, Captain Josiah Macy, moved from Nantucket to New York, where he founded the very successful shipping and commission house of Josiah Macy & Son. Kate's father, a member of the eighth generation of the family in America, became a close friend and business associate of John D. Rockefeller, whose Standard Oil Company had acquired the Macy family's New York oil-refining operation. As a result of his association with Rockefeller, Josiah Macy Jr. significantly added to the family's already sizeable fortune before his untimely death, of typhoid fever, at age thirty-seven, when Kate was only thirteen.

In 1883 Kate Macy married Walter Graeme Ladd, the Brooklyn-born son of William Whitehead Ladd and Sarah Hannah Phillips Ladd. Walter Ladd was a merchant in the dried-fruit business and, later, the insurance business. He eventually gave up his outside business pursuits and focused on caring for his sickly wife and managing their investments and estates in New Jersey and Maine.

Kate Ladd was an invalid for much of her married life, spending many years in bed or a wheelchair. While the cause of her malady was disputed by her physicians and nurses, muscle atrophy eventually rendered her unable to walk. However, in her memoirs, she recalled that the first eight years she lived at *Natirar* were "the best days of my life in many ways—really the first time in my life that I had known what it was to be really well."

Natirar's *first-floor rooms featured elaborate plaster ceilings, teak floors, and extensive woodwork, as seen in these photographs of the billiard room (left) and library that were taken in 1912 as the house was nearing completion. The walls of the large living room were covered in carved oak linenfold paneling.*

Reared in a somewhat austere Quaker household, Kate was strongly influenced by the religion's spirit of humanitarianism and by her family's history of philanthropy. She had a generous and loving disposition and showed a genuine concern for the welfare of others. The close bonds she developed with her physicians and other caregivers had a profound influence on her philanthropic endeavors.

She made substantial contributions—always anonymously or in memory of friends and family—to many charitable and educational organizations, including the Henry Street Settlement in New York, the Maine Seacoast Missionary Society, the YWCA, the Hospital Council of New York City, the Berry Schools in Rome, Georgia, and the United Hospital Fund. Local organizations also benefited from her charity, including the Visiting Nurse Association of Somerset Hills, the Bernardsville Library, and what is now the Somerset Medical Center in Somerville.

The most significant of Kate Ladd's philanthropic contributions was the creation, in 1930, of the Josiah Macy Jr. Foundation, named in honor of her beloved father. By the time of her death, in 1945, Mrs. Ladd had given the foundation about $19 million—a huge sum in today's dollars. Initially supporting medical research, the foundation has focused its resources since the 1960s on improving the education of health professionals, particularly physicians.

Walter Ladd died twelve years before his wife, and under the terms of his will, the Kate Macy Ladd Fund was set up to ensure the continuation of what his wife considered to be her most important project—a convalescent home for women. In 1908 Mrs. Ladd had established such a facility on the *Natirar* estate, originally at *Maple Cottage*, a large home on Peapack Road that has been demolished. Its mission was: "Deserving gentlewomen who are compelled to depend upon their own exertions for support shall be entertained, without charge, for periods of time while convalescing from illness, recuperating from impaired health, or otherwise in need of rest."

Walter Ladd's will specified that after Kate's death title to *Natirar* was to be conveyed to the fund and the convalescent facility was to be relocated from *Maple Cottage* to the renovated main residence. The Kate Macy Ladd Home operated there from 1949 until 1983, the fiftieth anniversary of Walter Ladd's death. That year, in accordance with his will, the remaining 500-acre property was sold, purchased by His Majesty Hassan II, the King of Morocco, for $7.5 million. The principal of the Kate Macy Ladd Fund was then distributed equally among five organizations: New York University, Johns Hopkins Hospital, Tuskegee College in Alabama, Hampton Institute in Virginia, and the Berry Schools in Georgia. King Hassan died in 1999, and three years later Somerset County acquired the historic estate, much of it to be set aside for public use.

The North Branch of the Raritan River flows for two miles across the Natirar estate. Large stretches of the riverbank were originally lined with fitted stone walls to control erosion. The river and estate could be viewed from the several bridges and the miles of drives that crossed the 1,000-acre property.

BEDMINSTER

Homestead of Johannes Moelich family, built 1752.

HAMILTON FARM

The story of *Hamilton Farm* is a tale of great wealth and grand design. At its zenith, *Hamilton Farm* sprawled across nearly 5,000 acres in three counties. Here, in the first decades of the twentieth century, James Cox Brady (1882–1927) created a resplendent country estate and one of the largest working farms in New Jersey.

Hamilton Farm mirrored the expansive nature of its owner. Brady, a Yale–educated New York financier, was the grandson of an Irish immigrant and son of Anthony Nicholas Brady, who had made a fortune in utilities. Brady was known for his competitive spirit and keen desire to excel. At the farm, he established a way of life that the family could not have achieved in Ireland. *Hamilton Farm* was built in the manner of the great country homes of England. It was as though Brady sought to exceed in scope and grandeur the lifestyle of the absentee English landlords who had caused his Irish forebears to lead such a wretched existence.

After the turn of the century, when other wealthy New Yorkers were building palatial homes in the hills of Morris County and Bernards Township, Brady looked west to the green fields and woodlands of Bedminster. He was introduced to the area by his friend Charles Pfizer, son of the pharmaceutical magnate, who brought the Essex Hunt to the area. Brady's first land purchase, in 1911, was a 190-acre farm adjoining Pfizer's Gladstone property, acquired for $100 per acre. He named the farm for his first wife, Elizabeth Jane Hamilton. He bought many other farms in the succeeding years. Ultimately, *Hamilton Farm* reached into Morris, Somerset, and Hunterdon counties.

Construction at the farm began in 1912. The first building completed was the lodge, located along the main drive and used by the Brady family during the hunting season for brief visits to the farm. The main house, a long clapboard structure designed by Henry Otis Chapman of the New York architectural firm of Barney & Chapman, was sited on a knoll overlooking formal gardens and a greenhouse. The house was handsome and spacious but not as palatial as many of the residences on the Bernardsville mountain. Close by the house, Brady built an athletic building, with a squash court, a fifty-foot tiled pool, and indoor and outdoor tennis courts.

Aerial view of Hamilton Farm *taken sometime prior to 1923, the year the original residence was destroyed by fire. In the foreground are the main house and original greenhouse; upper left are the barns; upper right is the stable, which, since 1961, has been the home of the United States Equestrian Team; right are the chicken houses and kennels; center are the greenhouses.*

The farm buildings were screened from the residence by a stand of trees. The horse barn, bull barn, and blacksmith shop were completed in 1913. About three years later, the huge cow barn and the lavish fifty-four-stall horse stable were finished. The farm became a vast operation. More than 4,000 acres were cultivated. Corn, wheat, oats, rye, and hay were harvested. Dairy and beef cattle, sheep, pigs, chickens, ducks, and geese were raised at *Hamilton Farm.* One hundred or more men were regularly employed, exclusive of the staff in the main house or extra laborers hired for construction. The farm payroll ranged between $4,000 and $8,000 a month, at a time when only the farm manager and foreman earned more than two dollars a day.

Management of the farm was under the careful eye of Fred Huyler, who held the job for fifty years. Huyler, a Peapack carpenter, was singled out by Brady to help him acquire the land, develop the farm, erect the houses, barns, stables, and kennels, and buy, breed, and exhibit the livestock, poultry, and dogs. A tight chain of command from Brady through Huyler to various employees kept the farm running smoothly. Huyler, a showman at heart, spent much of his time on the road successfully exhibiting the Brady Herefords, Jersey cows, Dorset sheep, Duroc-Jersey swine, chickens, and German shepherd dogs. Huyler

became an international authority on trailing hounds and breeding chickens. The Brady stock traveled to exhibitions and competitions by private train car. The animals were herded down the back farm drive directly to the Peapack station and loaded into specially outfitted cars. There was a festive air in the village when the parade of animals came to the station.

Original clapboarded Hamilton Farm *residence, which burned to the ground in 1923. A new brick house was soon built on the site. It was gutted by fire in 1978, and then rebuilt within the original walls (see pages 210–11).*

Ellen Biddle Shipman landscaped the rebuilt house for James Cox Brady in 1925. In the 1930s, after Brady's death, Shipman was retained by his widow, Helen, who had been remarried to C. Suydam Cutting, to carry out additional landscape work.

The Brady home burned to the ground in 1923. On its foundation, Brady built a new residence, a Georgian brick mansion with sixty-four rooms, eleven fireplaces, two elevators, and a chapel with stained-glass windows and an organ. The architects were Montague Flagg, a nephew of the prominent architect Ernest Flagg, and Christian F. Rosborg. Ellen Biddle Shipman, who has been hailed as "the dean of American women landscape architects," was commissioned to design the grounds of Brady's new house in 1925. Shipman was retained again in the 1930s by Brady's widow, Helen, who had been remarried to C. Suydam Cutting, to carry out additional landscape work.

Hamilton Farm flourished during the 1920s. The stable was filled with Hackney ponies, hunters, Clydesdales, and Percheron draft horses. In the greenhouses grew nectarines, pineapples, melons, and every sort of vegetable and flower. Homebred livestock were slaughtered and aged in the farm butcher shop. Milk, cream, and butter were produced at the creamery. The Brady's New York City house and yacht were stocked with provisions from the farm.

The farm was in every way a showplace. The new main residence was furnished with the finest antiques, carpeting, and works of art. The grounds and gardens were planted with specimen trees, bushes, and flowering plants. Farm machinery and equipment was the newest and most sophisticated available. Every animal was an outstanding specimen of its breed. An animal photographer was employed to take posed pictures and portraits of the animals.

The influence of *Hamilton Farm* on the community was profound. Employment was provided for a generation of local people and merchants prospered through endless orders for farm equipment and supplies. The lives of the people on the farm and in the neighboring villages were enhanced by their proximity to such splendid abundance.

Then suddenly it was over. When Brady died of pneumonia in 1927, his heirs closed down the entire farm operation and the animals were sold.

Much of the estate was sold during the years following Brady's death, although family members continued to live in the house and many still reside in the area. In 1978 a fire destroyed the mansion, causing the death of a Brady relative. That year Beneficial Management Corporation bought the mansion and more than 500 acres of *Hamilton Farm* for use as a corporate conference center. Architect J. Robert Hillier of the Hillier Group in Princeton was hired to rebuild the house within its original brick walls. Since then the property has changed hands several times and is now the 36-hole Hamilton Farm Golf Club.

Fifty-foot indoor pool located in the estate's athletic building, which also included squash and tennis courts.

Chapel.

Front hall.

Living room.

Dining room.

Front hall looking through library toward living room.

Library.

Hamilton Farm *sprawled over 5,000 acres in three counties, with 4,000 acres under cultivation and more than 100 people employed on just the farming operation.*

Sitting room of master bedroom suite.

HAMILTON FARM STABLE

Horses have always been an important part of life in the Somerset Hills, and there is no more spectacular monument to the love of horses than the opulent stable complex built by James Cox Brady at *Hamilton Farm*. Brady spared no expense to create an equestrian showplace for his prized Hackney ponies, hunters, and the Clydesdale and Percheron draft horses used to work the 5,000-acre farm.

Designed by New York architect William Weissenberger Jr., the stable complex was completed in 1917 at a cost of more than $250,000. Twenty-five men were employed to care for the horses and maintain the building, which was one of the grandest stables in the country.

The three-story structure was constructed of stucco over brick and reinforced with steel to make it fireproof. The building featured self-supporting tile ceiling vaults invented and installed by the Guastavino Fireproof Construction Company. The fifty-four varnished hardwood box stalls, each twelve feet square, had cork brick floors and flushable drains. But the stable was built to please human sensibilities as well as to provide comfort and protection for Brady's beloved horses. Among the unusual design features were an arched center entrance leading into an octagonal foyer, glazed tiled walls, floors of terrazzo brick laid in a herringbone pattern, and gleaming brass fixtures.

A second-story trophy room, located above a center rotunda, featured a spectacular Tiffany stained-glass ceiling, hand-carved walnut trophy cases and oak flooring. Brady's guests would gather around the railings of the rotunda to observe, through a decorative oval plate-glass floor, horses parading across a red carpet below. The stable originally had rooms for ten workers, an apartment for the stable manager, game rooms, and eight baths. Sculptors were brought over from Italy to craft three magnificent

Completed in 1917 at a cost of more than $250,000, the stable building at Hamilton Farm was one of the grandest in the country.

The Essex Fox Hounds meet at the Hamilton Farm *stable in the 1920s.*

bronze weather vanes for the building, one of which was modeled on Brady's favorite horse, Hamilton Model.

After Brady's death in 1927, his heirs shut down the farming operation and sold the animals. However, the stable got a new use in the 1940s when Brady's third wife, the remarried Helen McMahon Brady Cutting, suggested that the complex be converted into an emergency hospital for merchant marine seamen who had endured shipwrecks, torpedoing, and sea fatigue. The Hamilton Farm Base Hospital No. 1, complete with an operating room and capable of accommodating 200 patients, opened in 1942 and served about 5,000 patients before closing five years later. In 1943 the Duke and Duchess of Windsor, who had twice before been houseguests of Mrs. Cutting, visited the

hospital. The Cuttings also set up the Hamilton Farm Cannery, which canned vegetables and fruit grown on the estate and shipped them to beleaguered Great Britain.

In 1961 the stable was put to another use when the Brady family's landholding company entered into a lease with the United States Equestrian Team, which was looking for a headquarters and training center. The future of the USET at *Hamilton Farm* was placed into doubt in 1978, when Brady Security & Realty Corporation sold more than 500 acres—including the *Hamilton Farm* main house, stable complex, and outbuildings—to the Beneficial Management Corporation. However, Beneficial proved to be a generous benefactor, donating the stables and 7.5 surrounding acres to the USET in 1988.

Top: Cross hall showing glass floor of trophy room above.

Above, left: Carriage house.

Above: Exercise ring behind the stable.

Left: The stable had fifty-four varnished box stalls, each twelve feet square, with cork brick floors, flushable drains, and ornamental finials. Overhead was a self-supporting Guastavino vaulted tile ceiling.

Second-floor trophy room with glass skylight and glass floor overlooks the stable's main cross hall.

Cross hall with glass floor of trophy room above, Guastavino tile ceiling, and glazed-brick walls.

GREENACRES

Just over the hill and across the fields from the Essex Fox Hounds is a sprawling country estate built around 1910 for Frederic Bull (1871–1948)—a World War I army captain and board chairman of the Oriental Consolidated Mining Company—his first wife, Helen Robinson, and their daughter, Frederica, the grandmother of the renowned opera singer Frederica von Stade. The Bulls' house, which they called *Brookhills Farm*, was built on the site of a mid-nineteenth-century farmhouse owned by Martin Latourette, the son of early farming settlers in Bedminster, Cornelius and Elizabeth Wyckoff Latourette.

In 1916 the property was bought by William Vincent Griffin (1886–1958), a financial advisor to James Cox Brady. Griffin and Brady met as undergraduates at Yale, where they established a lifelong friendship. Griffin eventually become chairman of the Brady family's landholding company, Brady Security & Realty Corporation, and was a trustee of Brady's estate following the latter's premature death in 1927 at the age of forty-five. Thirty-one years later, Brady's son, James Cox Brady, acted as executor of Griffin's estate. Griffin held more than a dozen directorships, including those of the Chase Manhattan Bank, Continental Oil Company, Purolator Products, Emigrant Industrial Savings Bank, Central Railroad of New Jersey, and Time Inc., where he was one of the original directors, serving in that role for thirty-five years. He was also a member and vice chairman of the New Jersey Racing Commission.

Griffin married Isabel Carden whose sister was married to Wing Commander Gerald Constable Maxwell of the Royal Air Force, a tie that bound the Griffins to England throughout their lives. The Griffins hosted many prominent English guests at *Greenacres*—the name they gave to their estate—including Field Marshal Viscount Bernard L. Montgomery, commander in chief of the British armies on the western front in World War II, who was a frequent visitor. During the war, the Griffins' English nephews and nieces were sent out of the country and spent long periods at *Greenacres*.

Griffin served as president of the prestigious English Speaking Union for ten years. In 1952 he was made an honorary Knight Commander of the Order of the British Empire by Queen Elizabeth II in recognition of his con-

tribution to promoting relations between people of the English-speaking world.

The Griffins carried out extensive renovations to their estate. The noted architect Francis Burrall Hoffman Jr., who for a time rented the adjacent property, the *Spook Farm*, was commissioned to draw up the plans. The landscaping was by Ruth Bramley Dean, who planned formal gardens with hedges of English box. *Greenacres* had many fine features including a library with raised paneling of polished walnut and an antique carved-pine boiserie in the living room. The 200-acre property was run as a farm, including the breeding of Percheron draft horses. The estate's outbuildings, which conform in style to the main house, include a magnificent stable courtyard and adjoining barn. A capstone on the original part of the barn reads "M.L. 1843," dating it to the original owner of the property, Martin Latourette.

Isabel Griffin and her husband were deeply religious, though of different denominations, she an Episcopalian and he a Catholic. William Griffin was a prominent layman and gave many hours of service to his local church, St. Brigid's in Peapack, and to the Vatican, where he spent two weeks every other year in service. Griffin's honors from the Vatican included Knight Commander of the Order of St. Gregory; Papal Chamberlain Cape and Sword; Knight of Malta; and Knight Official of the Crown of Italy. Isabel was an invalid and bedridden for much of her adult life, so an altar was set into an alcove in her bedroom. After her death in 1954, Griffin donated candlesticks in her memory to her Peapack parish, St. Luke's. *Greenacres* was sold soon after Griffin's death in 1958. As stipulated in his will, much of the proceeds were donated to the Catholic Church.

Architect Francis Burrall Hoffman Jr. designed extensive alterations for William and Isabel Griffin after they purchased the property in 1916. Ruth Bramley Dean was the landscape architect. The sculpture is Venus Anadyomene *by Paul Manship.*

Built in 1910 by W. F. Haskew of Gladstone for Henry and Julia Lance, the house was originally called Lancecote. *William Thorn Kissel and his wife, Frances Dallett Kissel, acquired the property from the Lances in 1917 and renamed it* October House.

OCTOBER HOUSE

Near the end of World War I, New York investment banker William Thorn Kissel (1886–1960) was looking for a country home, and *October House* was the perfect choice. The imposing estate on Holland Road straddling what are today Bedminster and Peapack-Gladstone, abutted the Essex Fox Hounds property. Like many wealthy men of his era, Kissel had a passion for horses—not only foxhunting, but also polo, which he is credited with introducing to Bedminster.

William Thorn Kissel was descended from a family of great wealth and dynamism. His maternal great-grandfather was the transportation magnate and philanthropist Commodore Cornelius Vanderbilt, who made a vast fortune in the steamer and, later, the railroad businesses. William Thorn's father, Gustav Edward, was a highly successful investment banker who, in 1906, formed the firm of Kissel, Kinnicutt & Company, in partnership with G. Hermann Kinnicutt. The firm later merged with Kidder, Peabody & Company. In 1904 Gustav Kissel built one of the most outstanding estates ever to grace Morristown's Washington Valley, *Wheatsheaf Farms*. For many years after Gustav's wife's death in 1949, the mansion served as a retreat for the Sisters of the Good Shepherd, who conveyed the property to an affiliate of the Kessler Assisted Living Corporation in 1998, which resold the property in late 2001.

William Thorn Kissel, who worked as an investment banker in his father's firm, also served as director of the Standard Milling Company and of the Hudson Companies. He bought his country estate—then called *Lancecote*—in 1917 from an English couple, Henry W. Lance and his wife, Julia. The Lances had moved to the area in the early 1900s to hunt with Charles Pfizer's Gladstone drag hounds, precursors to the Essex Fox Hounds. In 1910 the Lances commissioned the residence, which was crafted in English Tudor style with non-structural timber beams and stucco-faced infill. W. F. Haskew of Gladstone is recorded as the builder. At the start of World War I, the Lances returned to England and Henry joined the British Army.

When Kissel purchased the property, it comprised 300 acres and encompassed the land on which the Frank Johnson residence, *Ellistan*, was later built. The interior of the house was somewhat austere with extensive wood paneling. It was perched on a hill, offering sweeping views of the property, which included a golf links. Kissel's wife, Frances Dallett, who loved the vibrant autumn foliage of the area, named the estate *October House*. The estate comprised staff cottages (see *Cherryfields*) and an eighteenth-century farmhouse in which Kissel's farm manager lived. To the southeast of the main house were the stables, which burned down in 1950. The adjacent carriage house and groom's quarters are now private residences, and what was the estate's icehouse is now a garage. The landscape architecture firm of Brinley & Holbrook of New York was retained to redesign the estate's gardens and grounds.

Not far from the old stables is a rectangular field that, in 1929, Kissel made into a polo field. The ground was uneven and the field undersized, but it was adequate for the scrub teams made up of Kissel, his friends, and neighbors. Although polo was introduced to the Somerset Hills in 1899 by Charles Pfizer who organized a club in Bernardsville, local interest in the sport significantly increased in the late 1920s when several local teams sprang up. There were the Peapack Blues, the Mine Mountain Hurricanes, the Burnt Mills Ramblers, and the Vliettown Four. On Sunday afternoons in the summer, up to sixty ponies would be led from the Essex Fox Hounds stables up the road to Kissel's field where spectators would gather, lining their vintage cars on the uphill side of the field. Many

would bring their backgammon boards, which was all the rage, and play when the action on the field was slow.

Schley Field in Bedminster was also used for polo games, with social gatherings held after the matches in the adjacent Jacobus Vandeveer house, which was owned by the Grant B. Schley family. So popular were the games that traffic congestion became a problem. In 1930, at a cost of about $75,000, Kissel and other members of the Essex Fox Hounds bought the 200-acre Nevius farm along the Lamington River near Pluckemin with level stretches large enough for three regulation polo fields. The Burnt Mills Polo Club was established and existed until the 1990s. Kissel's interest in the sport was more than local, however.

For many years he was a member of the governing board of the United States Polo Association.

Unlike her husband, Frances Dallett Kissel was a city aficionado. Although she had a racing stable and was a keen spectator of the sport, she did not particularly enjoy country pursuits, preferring to spend her time in the family's Manhattan residence. In 1942 the Kissels sold *October House* and made their permanent home in the city. One of their three children, Peter, took over his mother's race horses, naming his Pottersville stables *October House Farm* after his childhood home.

William Thorn Kissel died in May 1960, the day after his wife's death.

CHERRYFIELDS

ONE OF THE MOST CHARMING HOUSES in Peapack, *Cherryfields* was originally two separate cottages on the estate of investment banker William Thorn Kissel. Kissel's chauffeur occupied one and his gardener the other. In the mid-1930s the cottages and some surrounding acreage were purchased by Helen Stutzer Taylor. Helen and her sister, Elise Woodward Stutzer, hired A. Musgrave Hyde, a partner in the New York firm of architects Hyde & Shepard, to join the two houses. The sisters told Hyde that they wanted to dine together and visit each other by day, but they required privacy, too. The chauffeur's cottage was knocked down, rebuilt in brick, and joined to the 1840 timber-frame cottage by a glass walkway and an elegant high-ceilinged living room. Corinthian pilasters from a home in Trenton give the living room a classical dimension that has impressed the numerous style magazines that have photographed it over the years. In keeping with the wishes of the sisters, the two wings of the house were not connected upstairs.

Among *Cherryfields'* many delightful features are a window that faces out from one of the chimneys, intricate wrought-iron work on the entrance portico, and a dining room fireplace that came from Harriet Beecher Stowe's house in Hartford, Connecticut. A wisteria-covered arbor and terraces overlook lawns that slope steeply down to a long, narrow swimming pool, which Hyde designed for Helen Taylor's son, Corydon, a member of Dartmouth's swim team. Hyde fashioned an ornamental wall at the deep end of the pool, which doubles as a high-dive platform.

In the early 1950s the property was bought by diplomat Norman Armour (1887–1982), whose brother, William Armour, then lived in the converted brick barns at *Upton Pyne* in Bernardsville. Norman Armour, a career foreign service officer, served as an ambassador or minister to a dozen countries, including Canada, Belgium, Italy, France, Japan, Chile, Argentina, Venezuela, and Spain. In 1947 he capped his long career by being appointed assistant secretary of state for political affairs by President Truman.

Armour married Princess Myra Koudacheff of Petrograd, Russia, who—with Armour's help—escaped to Sweden during the Russian Revolution. The Armours named their home *Cherryfields* after two cherry trees planted in the garden.

Since 1955 the estate has been home to the John Pyne family. Pyne's wife, Nancy, is the daughter of Leonard J. Buck, whose acclaimed rock garden, once part of the Buck family's *Allwood* estate, is open to the public. Nancy Pyne inherited her father's passion and created beautiful gardens at her home, including an herb garden planted between the flagstones of a terrace.

PEAPACTON

T HE ESTATE OF *Peapacton* in Bedminster was purchased in 1914 by Rutherford Stuyvesant Pierrepont
(1882–1950), a coal company executive and banker, and
his wife, Nathalie de Castro, from Cecil Lyon and his wife,
Anita de Bary Lyon. The Pierreponts commissioned the
New York architect, Montague Flagg, a nephew of architect Ernest Flagg, to draw up plans for a country house. It
was Montague Flagg who, in the 1920s, was one of the
architects who designed a new *Hamilton Farm* residence for
James Cox Brady after the original house burned down.

The Pierreponts and Flagg chose a house site on the
property that afforded pleasant views across a valley to
hills beyond. *Peapacton*—a Native American word for "rip-
pling brook"—was completed in 1917. Flagg's design, a
long and irregular stucco structure with a slate roof, was
inspired by French country homes. Its unpretentious main
entrance and conical tower were reminiscent of the
estates of Normandy and Brittany. To the north of the
house was flatter land, perfect for the outbuildings that
were built as part of Pierrepont's working farm. The
handsome courtyard stable was designed in conformity
with the house. After World War I, in which Pierrepont
served as a first lieutenant and later captain in the Army
Air Service, the stable was used temporarily as a convalescent home for veterans. Later, Pierrepont converted a
room in the stable into an office to avoid traveling to the
city every day. The pool and Regency-style pool house
were designed by Frederick Godwin, a Pierrepont relative.
The large, high-ceilinged pool house was built into the
hillside to capture the views across the valley, while the
pool was designed to overflow, suggesting a natural spring.

Pierrepont was a descendant of the Rev. James Pier-
pont—one of the founders of Yale College—and of John
Jay, the first chief justice of the United States. Pierrepont
grew up in Brooklyn and was educated at Columbia University, where he also received a law degree. Although he
was admitted to the bar, Pierrepont never practiced law.

The north façade of Peapacton, *which was designed by Montague Flagg
for the Rutherford Stuyvesant Pierreponts and completed in 1917.*

Peapacton's *stables*.

He began his career as a mule-team operator with Keokee Consolidated Coal & Coke Company, one of the many companies of which he was later named a director. He also served as a director of Virginia Coal & Iron Company, Fidelity & Casualty Insurance Company, Franklin Trust Company of Brooklyn, Bank of America, and New York Trust Company, where he was employed in the trust department for many years. Pierrepont was a founding director of the China Society of America, established in 1914.

Pierrepont married Nathalie de Castro in 1911, and they lived in Manhattan until their move to the New Jersey countryside. Pierrepont was a dedicated sportsman, fond of shooting and fishing and foxhunting with the Essex Fox Hounds. Nathalie also hunted and loved dogs, which were raised in the kennels at *Peapacton*. The Pierreponts kept many varieties of bird dogs, including their beloved Irish setters. Pierrepont took an active interest in his farm, conducting inspection tours of the property on horseback. Beef cattle, hogs, and sheep were bred, and the farm came to be known for its modern agricultural methods.

After Pierrepont's death in 1950, Nathalie moved to Princeton, finding life as a widow in the country lonely. The main house and eighty acres were sold in 1958.

About half a mile down the road from the main house was an eighteenth-century farmhouse, which was part of Pierrepont's original purchase. The simple timber-frame structure had once been owned—and may well have been built—by the Sutphens, Dutch settlers who acquired considerable acreage in Bedminster and rose to positions of prominence in the community. Pierrepont used the house as a farm cottage for *Peapacton*. Later, it was rented out, but little was done over the years to improve it until after Pierrepont's death, when his son, John, moved in.

John Pierrepont and his wife, the former Nancy Weller, hired local architect James S. Jones to carry out extensive alterations to the house, including the addition of a servants' wing, a living room wing, a third floor, and separate guest quarters. A pool, tennis court, and stable were also built, although the stable later burned down and was not rebuilt. The elegant decorations and furnishings of the house were chosen by Nancy, an interior decorator.

John and Nancy Pierrepont sold the house in 1994. The new owners—who named the property *Peapacton Farm*—extensively remodeled and redecorated the residence, which was the subject of an eight-page article in the July 1997 issue of *Architectural Digest*.

The south façade of Peapacton overlooks sprawling fields.

The original land purchase by Rutherford Stuyvesant and Nathalie Pierrepont in 1914 included an eighteenth-century farmhouse of the Sutphen family. The house served as the farm cottage for Peapacton until the 1950s, when the Pierreponts' son, John, and his wife, Nancy, moved in and retained local architect James S. Jones to make extensive additions and alterations. The center section with dormer windows is the eighteenth-century core of the house. The property was sold by the Pierreponts in 1994 and renamed Peapacton Farm by the new owners. The house was featured in a major Architectural Digest *article in July 1997.*

WHITE OAKS

THIS EIGHTEENTH-CENTURY Bedminster farm-house served as a stagecoach stop during the colonial period. In 1908 Frank L. Stoutenburgh, who owned a fine-clothing establishment in Newark, purchased the house and 150 acres from Joseph Nevius, a descendant of the Dutch settler family, adding it to an adjoining parcel of about 150 acres he had acquired from Albert Amerman. Stoutenburgh lived in the house until his death, in 1916. That year, James Cox Brady bought the property, and shortly thereafter conveyed it to his friend and stockbro-ker Edward Welch Clucas (1880–1948). Clucas married Frederic and Helen Bull's daughter, Frederica, at about that time, and it has been said that Brady gave them the house as a wedding present.

Clucas was a classmate of Brady's at Yale. After gradu-ation he worked for two securities trading firms, Redmond & Company and Coffin & Company. In 1906 he and Joseph Gilman formed a Wall Street partnership, Gilman & Clucas. In 1919 Clucas established his own brokerage firm, E. W. Clucas & Company, where he was a senior partner until his death. Clucas held several directorships, including vice president and director of Brady Security & Realty Corporation, and president and director of the Whiteoaks Land Corporation in Somerville, New Jersey.

Before embarking on renovations to their house, the Clucases had it moved from the road into a grove of white oak trees at the top of the hill, thus giving the estate its name, *White Oaks*. The house was winched up the hill with the help of horses and a jack. A two-story wing as well as a distinctive teak-floored "ship room," made of bolted oak from the cabin of an old sailing vessel, were added. Clucas was a keen yachtsman, owning what was believed to be one of the largest yawls in existence, the *Manxman*. A chestnut-paneled stable as well as kennels with red-tile roofing were built, the latter to house Clucas's beagles. Clucas, a great sporting man, hunted his White Oaks Foot Beagles, the precursors to the Tewksbury Foot Bassets, until 1945. Known to many as "Unc," he did not like auto-mobiles, preferring instead to drive around in horse-drawn vehicles. The Clucases had three children, one of whom, Sara Worthington, was the mother of the interna-tionally renowned mezzo-soprano, Frederica von Stade.

After Clucas's death in 1948, *White Oaks* was sold to John Currence, a doctor. Much of the property was subdivided into building lots and sold. This prompted Bedminster to adopt the zoning ordinance that established five-acre zoning in much of the township.

Living room and stair hall.

Edward Welch Clucas, who was a serious sailing enthusiast, had a teak-floored "ship room" constructed of bolted oak beams from the cabin of an old sailing vessel.

APPENDIX

The photographs on the epigraph page and each of the town-divider pages portray some of the landmark buildings and activities that, along with the great country houses, came to characterize the golden era of the Somerset Hills. These buildings and activities are described below.

RAILROAD SERVICE
TO THE SOMERSET
HILLS AND THE
BERNARDSVILLE
RAILROAD STATION

REGULAR train service from Hoboken, Newark, and Summit to Bernardsville, which began in early 1872 and was extended to Far Hills, Peapack, and Gladstone in 1890, was critical to the development of the Somerset Hills mountain colony, and it has remained an important factor in the area's economy to this day.

The railroad line from Summit to Gladstone, although only twenty-two miles in length and never a major freight route, has had a remarkably complex history and several name changes. In 1865, the New Jersey Legislature chartered the Passaic Valley & Peapack Railroad Company, authorizing it to construct a line "from some point in the county of Union or the county of Essex, passing through the Township of Springfield into the Township of New Providence, near the village of New Providence, so up the Passaic Valley at or near Basking Ridge and so on to the village of Peapack in the County of Somerset." Two years later, the charter was amended to authorize the railroad to extend its line to an unspecified point in Hunterdon County between Milford and Frenchtown; and two years after that, the line was further authorized to build a bridge over the Delaware River to connect to railroads in Pennsylvania and provide a freight route for Pennsylvania coal to reach the New York market. As a result of these charter amendments, the original name of the railroad no longer reflected its proposed scope of operations, and in 1870 the Legislature changed the name to the New Jersey West Line Railroad.

That same year, construction on the line was started at Summit, running west toward Somerset County. According to Thomas Townsend Taber in *The Delaware, Lackawanna & Western Railroad in the Nineteenth Century: 1828–1899*, the original intent was for the line to run through Liberty Corner, in Bernards Township, then on to

Peapack. It was later decided that the route should pass through Basking Ridge and Bernardsville because of the greater traffic potential. Although locomotives made test runs on the line in December 1871, it appears that regular passenger service began in early 1872—the first published timetable appeared in the February 10, 1872, issue of *The Jerseyman*, a Morristown newspaper of the day.

Within a couple of years, however, the railroad's financial backers decided on an alternate route to access the Pennsylvania coal fields. Plans to continue the line westward were shelved, and with the loss of revenue, the New Jersey West Line soon went into bankruptcy. In 1878 the line was sold to a representative of the Delaware, Lackawanna & Western Railroad, and a new company, the Passaic & Delaware Railroad, was formed to be the successor to the New Jersey West Line. Bernardsville resident Percy Rivington Pyne, the owner of *Upton Pyne*, served as one of the original directors of the Passaic & Delaware. Although the "P. & D.," as it was known, was operated as virtually a segment of the Delaware, Lackawanna & Western Railroad's Morris & Essex line—today's Morristown line of New Jersey Transit—it was not formally leased to the D. L. & W. until 1882.

In 1890 the short-line Rockaway Valley Railroad that ran from Whitehouse Station, where it connected to the Central Railroad of New Jersey, to Gladstone was being extended to Mendham and on toward Morristown. Although the Rockaway Valley's freight business hauling iron ore and peaches would plummet later that year because of a blight that largely wiped out the area's peach crop, the D. L. & W. nevertheless acted quickly to thwart the expected competition, organizing a new corporation, the Passaic & Delaware

Extension Railroad, to extend the P. & D.'s line from Bernardsville to Gladstone. No time was lost in building the seven-and-one-half-mile extension; the construction contract was awarded in April 1890 and work was completed only six months later. Although the P. & D.'s terminus at Gladstone was located less than one-half mile from the Rockaway Valley Line, the two railroads were never connected.

The landmark Bernardsville railroad station was built in 1901–02, replacing a smaller frame structure built thirty years before when the railroad was constructed from Summit. The quarry-faced ashlar stone station was designed by architect Bradford Lee Gilbert (1853–1911) in what has come to be known as the Richardsonian Romanesque style, after the influential architect, Henry Hobson Richardson. Gilbert's earlier proposed design for the station—which appears in a portfolio of watercolor renderings of Gilbert's work that was published in 1895—called for a smaller fieldstone structure with a round tower and half-timbering on the building's gable ends.

Although Gilbert was best known for his designs of railroad structures—he was a consulting architect to more than twenty railroads, and he remodeled the first Grand Central Depot in New York in 1892—he is also credited with being the first to design an entire building employing skeleton-frame construction technology that became the fundamental principle behind all modern skyscraper design. Before Gilbert's engineering breakthrough even the most advanced buildings had exterior walls that, because they supported themselves all the way up, had to increase in width toward the bottom. A 150-foot-high building required masonry walls three feet thick at the base.

In 1888, Noble Stearns, a silk importer who owned a lot on lower Broadway in New York only twenty-one feet, six inches wide, approached Gilbert "in despair." Stearns wanted to maximize the value of his property by constructing a tall commercial building, but he had been unsuccessful in acquiring the adjoining lots that would have given him the necessary "footprint" on which to build. Gilbert, because of his work designing railroad bridges and train sheds, determined that he could solve Stearns's problem and support both floors and exterior walls on a concealed iron skeleton, much like an iron bridge standing on end. The resulting structure, which required masonry walls only eight-to-twelve-inches thick, was the fifteen-story, 168-foot-high Tower Building at 50 Broadway, completed in 1889. The Tower Building, despite its relatively modest height and brief existence—it was demolished in 1914 after only twenty-five years—was a brilliant engineering feat that permitted the skyscrapers that now form the skyline of New York.

In Bernardsville, Gilbert's train station featured an interior with elegantly detailed waiting rooms with fireplaces, Corinthian pilasters carved in oak, and wood paneling. A regular supply of fresh flowers from the gardens and greenhouses on the Frederic P. Olcott estate, now the Somerset Hills Country Club, added a note of color.

Unlike most outmoded and replaced structures, the original wood-frame Bernardsville station did not suffer the usual fate of demolition. It was moved about a quarter-mile away where it briefly served as a school and today is the editorial office of *The Bernardsville News*, which has served as the weekly newspaper of the Somerset Hills since 1897.

THE SOMERSET INN

No SINGLE structure played a more important role in the development of the Somerset Hills as an area of country estates for New York and Newark society than the Somerset Inn. Most of those who came to build their luxurious "cottages" in the Bernardsville mountain colony between the 1870s and the early years of the twentieth century got their first exposure to the region as guests at the inn.

The nucleus of the building that evolved into the Somerset Inn started out as the summer home of a noted Methodist theologian, Bishop Edmund S. Janes (1807–1876), who

was among the first to introduce the Somerset Hills to prominent New Yorkers, many of whom were parishioners who visited him in Bernardsville. The word soon spread about the appealing summer climate and beautiful hilly environs, and in 1870 Bishop Janes's house and part of his homestead farm were acquired by Francis Oliver, who turned the white frame home into a summer boarding house that attracted increasing numbers of distinguished and well-to-do families, including New York architect George Browne Post (1837–1913) and banker George Ingraham Seney (1826–1893), both of whom soon began to acquire large tracts of land in the area.

In 1879 Seney, by then the president of the Metropolitan Bank in New York, acquired the Oliver boarding house property. Naming the old home of Bishop Janes the Highland House, Seney began to enlarge and improve it to become an exclusive, luxury resort hotel, with his own home—what later came to be called *The Maples*—located a short distance to the south.

The Highland House grew over the years to become a large frame building of eclectic design five stories high. It was described at the time as "a long, rambling, much-added-to [and] bewitchingly irregular structure that 'growed,' like Topsy." Set among large shade trees and surrounded by lawns and gardens, the property featured expansive views from what was nearly the highest point on the Bernardsville mountain. Advertisements in *The New York Times* emphasized the "pure, cool atmosphere and healthy surroundings" of the inn at an elevation that miraculously increased over the years from 800 to 1,000 feet above sea level!

Although the early guests of the Oliver boarding house generally arrived by carriage from Morristown, which then had the nearest train station, by early 1872 the railroad was constructed to Bernardsville, bringing more visitors to the area, many of whom decided to stay and build the estates that came to characterize the Somerset Hills for decades to come.

About 1887 Seney renamed the property the Somerset Inn. Open from the middle of May to late October, the inn soon became one of the most renowned and elegant hostelries on the Eastern Seaboard, accommodating more than 400 guests at a time. Advertisements in *The New York Times* and other publications dubbed Bernardsville "The Lenox of New-Jersey," a comparison to the elegant summer resort of the wealthy in the Berkshire Hills of western Massachusetts.

In 1893 George Seney died and his extensive property holdings, consisting of more than 1,000 acres, including the Somerset Inn, were acquired by the Somerset Land Company. Organized by Seney's son, Robert (1850–1923), the company soon came to be controlled by brothers Grant B. Schley (1845–1917) and Evander H. Schley (1838–1907) and was the area's first real estate development company.

No doubt recognizing the distinct advantages of the Somerset Inn as a tool to help sell their properties, the Schleys added several facilities that were much in vogue in late-nineteenth-century luxury resorts. One was a "casino," a term used in its Renaissance meaning of a pleasure house, which was a separate building used for dances, concerts, and other entertainments. The Schleys also built eight large, two-story cottages—each containing seven to twelve rooms—for guests who preferred to have greater privacy, although take their meals at the inn. Located nearby was a private nine-hole golf course with its own rustic, Adirondack-style club house, which complemented the inn's other recreational activities, including tennis and croquet courts and a bowling alley.

The property's brochures touted it as "the best equipped mountain hotel within a hundred miles of New York" and boasted of its many amenities, including an "excellent orchestra" and "parlors, a music room, a billiard room and café, a barber shop and a news stand, a post office, a long distance telephone and a telegraph office," also noting that a physician was in residence. To help sell the real estate in the area, guests were provided with maps detailing places of interest along scenic carriage and, later, automobile drives.

Another useful marketing tool was *The Bernardsville Hills*, a "semi-monthly" magazine published by the inn in 1905 and 1906. Although each issue included articles describing area sites and history, there was a heavy emphasis on the comings and goings and social and recreational activities of the wealthy denizens of the mountain colony.

In early May 1908, a fire of mysterious origin burned the Somerset Inn to the ground, leaving only the "twenty-odd great chimneys" and the eight surrounding cottages and other outbuildings. By far the largest fire in the area for many years before or after, the "mighty blaze" was said to have "lighted the countryside for miles around." In a sad coda to that fire, almost exactly twenty years later, another mysterious blaze destroyed the old clubhouse building on the inn's former golf course, destroying virtually the last vestige of what had been a vital part of the development of the Bernardsville mountain colony.

HILLTOP CHURCH

THE FIRST Presbyterian Church, better known in the area as Hilltop Church, has been an iconic image of Mendham since it was constructed in 1859–60. It is the fourth church building to occupy this visually commanding site since the first meeting house was constructed there in 1745.

In the early 1730s, a small, primitive log meeting house had been built at "Rocksiticus" (now spelled Roxiticus), a small settlement in the area now known as Ralston about one and one-half miles to the west of what, by the 1740s, became the town center of Mendham. This spartan meeting house was known as "God's Barn" because it lacked heat and glass in the four small shuttered windows. It was located on the north side of what is now Route 24 just east of the Ralston General Store. According to a history of the Hilltop Church, the congregation of the log meeting house at Roxiticus was most likely of the Congregational sect, as members of the Southold, Long Island, Congregational church had settled in that area. By the late 1730s, however, records of the New Brunswick Presbytery reflect the existence of a Presbyterian congregation.

By 1745 a doctrinal dispute had divided the Roxiticus meeting house, with some members moving west to Chester, while others set about constructing a new house of worship in Mendham. Spearheading the drive to relocate to Mendham was Ebenezer Byram, whose son, Eliab, was pastor of the Roxiticus meeting house and became the first pastor of the new Mendham church. The elder Byram, who had built the Black Horse Inn at the crossroads in Mendham in 1742, commissioned his friend, the master builder John Cary, from Bridgewater, to construct the first Hilltop Church. The structure was described as "eminently American—simple, severe, and practical," with sides covered in short cedar shingles, no spire or cupola, large double batten doors, and inside a high gallery around three sides of the sanctuary, and a small box-like pulpit "raised on a single pillar to a dizzy height, with an octagonal sounding board, extended like an extinguisher over it, threatening to put out the minister."

This first church building served as an isolation hospital for soldiers stricken with small-pox when the Continental Army camped near Morristown in 1777 and at Jockey Hollow in 1779–80. Nearly thirty young Revolutionary War soldiers are buried in the church's graveyard.

The second Hilltop Church was built in 1817, replacing the original, which had been used for nearly three-quarters of a century and was considered outmoded and undersized. The new structure was destroyed by fire in 1835, but only nine months later a new church, similar in size to the previous one, was completed. Only twenty-four years later, however, fire struck again and a new church—the present structure—had to be built.

The present Hilltop Church was designed and built by Aaron Hudson (1801–1888), who was born and died in Mendham. Hudson, who described himself in the 1850 census as a "carpenter-builder," is credited with the design and construction of several public structures and residences in the area from the late 1830s to the 1870s.

Hudson's first commission is said to have been the portico that was added in 1838 to the Phoenix House, originally a hostelry located across the Washington Turnpike, now Route 24, from the Black Horse Inn. The underlying building, a brick, Federal-style structure, was largely obscured by Hudson's massive two-tiered portico with its heavy, Greek-inspired entablature supported by square piers. Hudson's other work in Mendham included his own Greek Revival home on Hilltop Road and the sanctuaries for St. Mark's (Episcopal) and St. Joseph's (Roman Catholic) churches.

The present Hilltop Church also has interesting connections to two of the country's most prominent and influential architects of the late-nineteenth and early-twentieth centuries: George Browne Post (1837–1913) and Thomas Hastings (1860–1929), whose residential work is well represented in the Somerset Hills and in this volume.

Post, the architect of the New York Stock Exchange whose family settled in Bernardsville in the early 1870s and whose firm had more than thirty residential commissions in the Somerset Hills, was retained by Rev. Israel Williams Cochran to design renovations to the Hilltop Church—and perhaps also to Hilltop House, the church parsonage—in 1876–77. Hastings, whose New York firm, Carrère & Hastings, designed the New York Public Library and the *Blairsden* estate in Peapack, was the son of Rev. Thomas S. Hastings, who was pastor of Hilltop Church from 1852–56.

SOMERSET HILLS
COUNTRY CLUB

THE FIRST clubhouse of the Somerset Hills Country Club was designed by William Stone Post (1866–1940), son of the famed architect of the New York Stock Exchange, George Browne Post. The clubhouse was built in 1897–98 on the hill above Ravine Lake in what is now Far Hills. It was a rustic building, constructed of rough chestnut slabs and native stone that had been excavated from its foundation, and featured wide verandas on two levels overlooking the lake and an immense stone fireplace that rose from the floor to the open-raftered ceiling.

An article about the clubhouse that appeared in the mid-July 1905 issue of *The Bernardsville Hills*, a local periodical published by the owners of the Somerset Inn, described the view: "From the upper veranda a view of rare beauty greets the eye. In the distance Pickell Mountain breaks the horizon line, while forest and orchard and fields of ripened grass and golden grain lie between, giving color, variety and charm to the somnolent, irridescent landscape. The thick growth of trees almost submerges the club house.... Below, the waters of the lake curve about Laurel Hill like an inverted letter 'S,' making at one point the segment of an almost perfect circle." New York's *The Morning Telegraph* of February 27, 1910, opined that: "It would be hard to find a club which is more picturesquely situated and with such ideal surroundings."

The building was commissioned by The Ravine Association, a real estate corporation formed in 1896 by several prominent area residents. Two years before, they had acquired 365 acres—at a cost of about $80 an acre—along the North Branch of the Raritan River, in an area known as Hub Hollow, to develop the property as a country club. By 1897 the association had sufficient subscriptions to begin improving the property. In 1898–99 a stone dam was constructed to create Ravine Lake and provide for swimming, boating, and fishing; the clubhouse and adjacent nine-hole, 2,329-yard golf course, and grass and platform tennis courts and squash courts were built on the hilltop; and a network of roads, paths, and riding trails was laid out.

The first country club in America was named, appropriately, "The Country Club" and was established at Brookline, Massachusetts, in 1882. Four years later, Pierre Lorillard organized the Tuxedo Club at what is now Tuxedo Park, New York, one of the first exclusive country club-centered suburbs in the country. By the middle of the 1890s the first American golf boom was well underway, with golf courses being constructed throughout the country. The United States Golf Association was formed in 1894. By 1929, less than fifty years after the opening of The Country Club at Brookline, there were 4,500 country clubs across the United States.

The Somerset Hills Country Club was organized in 1899 for "social, intellectual and recreative purposes." The club leased the lake and boathouse, golf course, tennis courts, clubhouse, and other improvements from The Ravine Association year-to-year. By 1915, however, with club membership increasing and play on the tight nine-hole golf course getting congested, if not dangerous, the club members decided that an eighteen-hole course was desirable. Because suitable additional land was not available contiguous to the original course, the club relocated to its present location in 1918 on the former Frederic P. Olcott estate in Bernardsville, where an eighteen-hole course was laid out.

The new clubhouse was designed by the New York architectural firm of Lord & Hewlett, which designed several houses in the Somerset Hills. The new golf course was designed by Albert Warren Tillinghast (1874–1942), a colorful and flamboyant character, and extremely talented golf-course architect, who built or reconstructed about 200 courses across the country during a thirty-year career from 1909 to 1940, including the famed Upper and Lower courses at Baltusrol Golf Club in Springfield, New Jersey, and the Winged Foot Golf Club in Westchester County, New York.

In 1919 the Somerset Hills Country Club's original clubhouse above Ravine Lake, and about 110 surrounding acres, which included most of the original nine-hole course, was sold by The Ravine Association to Percy Rivington Pyne, whose estate, *Upton Pyne*, abutted the club's property. Pyne demolished the old clubhouse and, near its site, built a new home, called *Dogwood Hill*, for his eldest son, Grafton Howland Pyne. Soon thereafter, *Dogwood Hill* was destroyed by fire and a new house, now known as *Cragwood*, was immediately rebuilt on its site.

COACHING IN THE
SOMERSET HILLS:
C. LEDYARD BLAIR
DRIVING *DEFIANCE*

COACHING and other equestrian pursuits were central to the life of the Somerset Hills mountain colony from the very beginning. As Allison Wright Post, a son of architect George B. Post, wrote in *Recollections of Bernardsville New Jersey: 1871–1941*: "For some years before 1905, the number of owners of carriage and saddle horses, thoroughbreds of the finest kind, made Bernardsville remarkable. . . . At that time there were at least five four-in-hands to be seen driven by their owners; . . . a large number for so small a community." Among the local "cottagers" whose equipages included the large and impressive "four-in-hands"—coaches pulled by four horses in tandem pairs and rigged to be handled by a single driver—were Walter P. Bliss, Frederic and Seymour Cromwell, Edward T.H. Talmage, and Clinton Ledyard Blair.

While the majority of those who drove four-in-hand coaches were men, a number of women also enjoyed the sport. One, Helen Benedict Hastings, the wife of Thomas Hastings—the architect who designed Blair's Peapack estate, *Blairsden*—and the sister of Martha Benedict Turnbull of *Appletrees* in Bernardsville, was sometimes called "the best four-in-hand driver in this country," and she took many blue ribbons at the National Horse Show.

Ledyard Blair was, like most of the other prominent residents of the Somerset Hills, an avid horseman and coaching enthusiast. An early photograph of *Blairsden's* brick coach barn shows at least ten carriages and sleighs of various types and sizes. Blair's collection included the elegant "primrose-red" four-in-hand coach, the *Defiance*, which could hold as many as fourteen passengers.

Two factors that emerged in Europe near the end of the eighteenth century, the widespread use of spring suspensions on carriages and improved road surfaces, helped turn coaching from simply a utilitarian, and usually uncomfortable, means to get from one point to another into an elite sport requiring great skill that was seen as a pleasurable activity for its own sake. The first associations of amateur coachmen, the Bensington Driving Club and the Four-Horse Club, were formed in England in the first decade of the nineteenth century and were the forerunners of many aristocratic clubs that were organized on both sides of the Atlantic for those interested in driving as a recreational and competitive activity.

The earliest such club in the United States was the Coaching Club, formed in New York in 1875. According to Reginald W. Rives, a famous "whip," or driver, who wrote a history of the club in 1935 and also served as its president—and whose son, Reginald B. Rives, was the mayor of Peapack-Gladstone from 1930 to 1944—coaching as a pastime was introduced to the United States by Colonel Delancey Astor Kane in the 1870s with his beautiful cream and black four-in-hand, the *Tally-ho*. As the first such coach to be seen in America, the *Tally-ho* prompted many people erroneously to call all roofed vehicles drawn by four horses by that name.

Ledyard Blair was elected a member of the Coaching Club in 1903, and the next year hosted the club's annual drive, a three-day coaching trip from New York to *Blairsden* and back. These events, of which there were sometimes two per year, began in 1878. Reportedly, the club's longest annual drive took place in 1894, a four-day (one-way), 317-mile trip from New York to *Shelburne Farms*, the Dr. William Seward Webb estate near Burlington, Vermont.

The annual drives were elaborate affairs, expensive to mount and logistically challenging, requiring numerous changes of horses along the way. For example, a couple of days before the club's May 1904 drive from New York to *Blairsden*, six teams of four matched horses had to be positioned at stables along the route, along with the grooms necessary to care for them, and the guests' luggage had to be transported to the overnight destination at *Blairsden*. In coaching, speed did not count as much as style. The coaches, horses, and harness, as well as the boots and buttons of the drivers, were polished to a mirror finish, and every aspect of the enterprise was scrutinized.

The 1904 drive to *Blairsden* on the *Defiance* began at the Metropolitan Club at Fifth Avenue and Sixtieth Street in New York, crossing the Hudson River on the Pennsylvania Railroad ferry from West Twenty-third Street to Jersey City, then south to Bayonne, two ferries to Elizabeth, then northwest through Springfield to Madison, and continuing on through Morristown and Mendham to *Blairsden*. The trip took eight hours, including six stops along the way to change horses—a total of twenty-eight horses were required for the trip—and a two-hour lunch break provided by Hamilton McKown Twombly at his estate, *Florham Farms*, in Madison. Blair's guests were entertained at *Blairsden* that evening and the following day before returning to New York on the *Defiance*, with a lunch stop at the Morristown Club on the way.

The following year, and again in 1907 and 1910, Blair hosted Coaching Club drives from New York to *Blairsden*, sometimes varying the trip by an extra day to include an outbound detour through Tuxedo, New York. The club's fall 1909 drive uniquely combined two of Blair's favorite pastimes, coaching and yachting. He invited the participants in the two-day drive from New York to Alfred Gwynne Vanderbilt's Newport estate, *Oakland Farm*, to dine with him and stay overnight on his 256-foot steam yacht, the *Diana*, which was moored for the occasion at New London, Connecticut.

In addition to the annual drives, the Coaching Club held an annual "parade" in New York's Central Park. These thrilling events usually involved twelve or more "drags," another term for four-in-hand coaches, although usually lighter, and thereby faster, than the original English models. The coaches, each with a complement of a dozen or more elegantly dressed guests, would process through the park then drive north to Jerome Park or Morris Park, elegant racetracks in the Bronx, for lunch.

Coaching declined as the use of automobiles increased and roads had to be shared with the noisy, smoke-belching machines. Allison Wright Post, in *Recollections of Bernardsville*, noted that at about the time the new railroad station was built in Bernardsville in 1901-02, "one began to notice a decided change from the use of horses and carriages to automobiles. Soon one was no longer conspicuous if he drove or was driven to the railroad station in an automobile." This change was not without its detractors, however. An anonymous Bernardsville summer resident wrote in a 1902 letter to the editor of *The New York Times*: "In view of the many recent, unnecessary and heart rending accidents caused by the reckless driving of automobiles, some action should be taken by the authorities . . . if they do not wish to drive people from Bernardsville as a 'dangerous place.'" The writer's recommendation was that automobiles, like the railway or trolley, "should be confined to tracks or special roads, limited to their use and protected by fences and gates at crossings."

Most of Ledyard Blair's coaches, carriages, and sleighs, including the *Defiance*, came to be owned by his daughter and son-in-law, Edith and Richard Van Nest Gambrill, who kept them at their own Peapack estate, *Vernon Manor*. Richard Gambrill, who was a serious horseman, coachman, and houndman, even co-authored a book, *Sporting Stables and Kennels* (Derrydale Press, 1935), with *Vernon Manor's* architect, James C. Mackenzie, about the proper way to design, construct, and equip stables, kennels, and coach barns.

Fortunately, most of the Blair and Gambrill coaches, carriages, and sleighs survive. Some, including the *Defiance*—repainted in black and red, the colors of the Gambrill stable—were donated by Edith Gambrill to her friend, Electra Havemeyer Webb, for display in Webb's Shelburne Museum in Vermont. Other Blair and Gambrill carriages and sleighs have found their way to the collection of the Staten Island Historical Society at Historic Richmond Town.

THE SOMERSET HILLS IN THE EIGHTEENTH CENTURY: THE MELICK HOMESTEAD

T HE MOELICH—later Anglicized to Melick and Mellick—homestead on Old Dutch Road in Bedminster has been a much-chronicled local landmark for more than 250 years. The property's site, however, located near the confluence of the North Branch of the Raritan River and the Peapack Brook, has been the scene of human transit, habitation, and industry far longer, first by American Indians and, since at least the 1730s, by European settlers.

Andrew D. Mellick Jr., in his classic 1889 book, *The Story of an Old Farm, or Life in New Jersey in the Eighteenth Century* (reissued in an edited version in 1948 under the title, *Lesser Crossroads*), noted that the area around his ancestral family farmstead "has produced a generous crop of stone implements and arrowheads" left by Native Americans who, for obvious practical reasons, no doubt resided in the vicinity of the two waterways. An important Indian path that later became one of the first roads in the area also crossed the property.

A. Van Doren Honeyman in his multi-volume work, *Northwestern New Jersey: A History of Somerset, Morris, Hunterdon, Warren and Sussex Counties*, wrote: "There appear to have been two preeminently important Indian paths . . . in the early days, both beginning at the sea-shore; the one over the Watchung Mountains near what is now Plainfield, and thence following the Passaic River northerly to the vicinity of modern Bernardsville; the other via 'Brunswick' and Somerville to Pluckemin and Peapack."

By the early 1730s an "improved" road—known as the "Peapack Path," the "Landing Road" or the "Bound Brook-Black River Road"—had been established over the route of this old trail that had connected northwestern New Jersey to points south and east near New Brunswick. The route of the Peapack Path was later followed by U.S. Route 202 north from Somerville through Pluckemin and on to "Lesser Cross Roads" in Bedminster. From there, the route continued up what is Hillside Avenue, then east on Old Dutch Road, crossing the Peapack Brook, then turning north and running slightly to the west of the present Peapack Road along the crest of the long, narrow ridge—known as the "Hogback"—between the Raritan River and the Peapack Brook and on to Peapack and Pottersville.

Despite the road's establishment in the early 1730s, permanent European settlement in the vicinity of the confluence of the two waterways did not begin for another ten years. The delay was caused, in large part, because of disputes over ownership of the land, a widespread and chronic problem in New Jersey during the period.

The area near the confluence of the Raritan and the Peapack Brook was once part of a 10,000-acre tract encompassing much of what is today Bedminster Township and the boroughs of Peapack-Gladstone and Far Hills. The land was purchased in 1701 by John Johnston and George Willocks from the East Jersey Proprietors, an association of twenty-four investors who had acquired Sir George Carteret's title to East New Jersey. The tract was later called the "Peapack Patent," named after the Peapack Path that crossed the property, and has since been the foundation of many land titles in the area.

In late 1751 Johannes Moelich, a tanner who had emigrated to America from Germany in 1735, purchased 367 acres within the Peapack Patent from George Leslie, a descendant of George Willocks, for a price that Andrew Mellick calculated at $2,369.44, or about $6.45 per acre. The original Melick tract ran from about the present-day Lamington Road on the south, to U.S. Route 206 on the west, and the Peapack Brook on the east.

A year after purchasing the property, the Melicks completed the construction of a permanent home built of red sandstone quarried on the property, replacing a thatched roof log home built the previous year. Although altered and enlarged somewhat during the first half of the twentieth century with the addition of dormer windows, a side porch, a clapboarded wing to the rear, and a kitchen wing with lean-to roof on the side, the Melicks' elegantly simple and solid stone homestead still proudly stands on the hill above Old Dutch Road.

In addition to farming, Melick practiced the craft of leather tanning that he had pursued in Germany. Soon after completing his new house, he built a tannery and bark mill—bark being a necessary ingredient in the tanning process—along the west side of the Peapack Brook across from a gristmill and sawmill that had been established by other early settlers. The family's tanning operation, which grew to include eighteen vats for soaking hides, continued well into the second half of the nineteenth century.

In the 1760s additional waterpower was required to drive the three mills that were clustered along the lower stretch of the Peapack Brook. The solution lay a quarter of a mile to the north where the Raritan River and the Peapack Brook came within 300 feet of each other.

Although the idea of diverting water from the Raritan to increase the flow of the Peapack Brook was an obvious one, the engineering challenge was contending with the long narrow hill, the Hogback, that separated the two waterways. To meet the challenge, a low dam was built across the Raritan just north of today's railroad bridge, creating a reservoir to facilitate a steady flow of water through a 500-foot channel that was built between the two waterways. For most of its length, the channel was an open trench, or race. However, at its upper end, where it was blocked by the Hogback, it took the form of a 100-foot-long tunnel, six-feet high and three- to four-feet wide, all excavated by hand through rock. At the midpoint of the tunnel were two right-angled turns that resulted from the tunnel's having been excavated simultaneously, and inaccurately, from both ends. Despite this underground miscalculation, the project was an impressive engineering success, accomplished ten years before the start of the American Revolution.

As Andrew Mellick noted in *The Story of an Old Farm,* "with the strange fatality that often attaches to local nomenclature in rural communities," the tunnel soon took on the sobriquet of "Hunt's Folly," after the engineer, Stephen Hunt, who helped create it. What has never been clear is whether the term "folly" referred to the engineering mistake that resulted in the twists of the water tunnel, or to the financial ruin that came to the owners of the downstream gristmill who underwrote the expensive project. In any event, the name "Hunt's Folly" stuck, even appearing more than a century later on the 1873 map of Bedminster Township in F. W. Beers's *Atlas of Somerset Co. New Jersey*.

The Melick homestead remained in family ownership for nearly 150 years. In 1893 it was sold at auction by the Somerset County Sheriff to Louisa Arrosmith Schomp, whose family had long owned the gristmill and sawmill on the opposite side of the Peapack Brook. Two years later, Mrs. Schomp sold the Melick property to Winslow Shelby Pierce, a prominent New York lawyer with Dillon & Hubbard, the firm in which John F. and John M. Dillon of Far Hills were partners. At the time, Pierce was handling the reorganization of the Union Pacific Railroad Company. He and the Dillons also served as counsel for the railroad magnate, Jay Gould.

In 1901, Pierce sold the property to Brigadier General Charles McCormick Reeve, the brother of Mrs. William T. Schley and an uncle of Reeve Schley, who was former New Jersey Governor Christine Todd Whitman's grandfather. General Reeve had a remarkably varied career. He was decorated for bravery in the Spanish-American War, and afterward served as the first prefect of military police in the Philippines. In addition to his military service, Reeve was at different times an attorney, banker, manager of manufacturing plants, Minnesota state legislator, author, singer, and philanthropist. He died in 1947 at age ninety-nine.

In 1914, General Reeve and his wife sold their 133-acre property to Kate Macy and Walter Graeme Ladd, whose nearly 1,000-acre *Natirar* estate came to include almost all of Johannes Moelich's 367-acre farm. The Ladds soon conveyed the Melick homestead and a small surrounding acreage to Mrs. Ladd's nephew, Josiah Macy Willets, and his wife, the former Gladys Bloodgood, a sister of Mrs. Charles Scribner Jr. After Mr. Willets's death in 1940, his widow kept the Bedminster property until 1947. Since that time the property has had several owners and has been carefully maintained.

ACKNOWLEDGMENTS

IN MANY WAYS this book was decades in the making, even though the actual research, photography, and writing was largely accomplished over the past three years. We both spent our formative years in the Somerset Hills, growing up on properties that were once part of two estates featured in this and the subsequent volume, and we have come to share a passionate interest in the area's history and rich architectural heritage. Despite that abiding interest, a work of this magnitude could not have been undertaken without the help of many others.

We realize it will be impossible to name everyone who assisted us in this project, and we humbly apologize in advance to those we may have inadvertently failed to identify. Fortunately, we will have the luxury of correcting at least some of those oversights in the next volume!

The present is truly enriched by an understanding of the past, and the archival collections in many of the area's libraries and historical societies are essential to the preservation and interpretation of our shared heritage. These collections, although a fragile and at-risk resource, comprise valuable treasure troves that are deserving of our protection and generous support.

Most importantly, our thanks and gratitude are extended to the staff of the Edwin S. Spinning Local History Room of the Bernardsville Public Library, particularly to Marion Kennedy, Jean Hill, Maud Thiebaud, Laura Cole, and Eileen Johnston, as well as the library's director, Karen Yanetta. Without the generous help, encouragement, and guidance of the knowledgeable and dedicated volunteers at the library who share our interest in local history, this book would not have been possible.

We also wish to thank some of the many people at several other libraries and historical societies who helped us, including Gustav Bittrich and the late Anne and Donald Q. O'Brien at the Clarence Dillon Public Library in Bedminster; Janet Castelpietra and Diane Deutsch at the Peapack-Gladstone Public Library; Christine Jochem and her staff in the local history and genealogy department at the Joint Free Public Library of Morristown and Morris Township; Valerie Komor at the New-York Historical Society; Chad Leinaweaver and Sally Yerkovich at the New Jersey Historical Society; Eileen Kennedy-Morales at the Museum of the City of New York; Charles F. Cummings at the Newark Public Library; Ulysses Grant Dietz at the Newark Museum; the Historical Society of the Somerset Hills; Susan Clark at the Mendham Borough Library; David Mitros at the Morris County Heritage Commission; Sara Weissman at the Morris County Library; the many superb research librarians at the New York Public Library; and Janet Parks and Louis DiGennaro at the Avery Architectural and Fine Arts Library at Columbia University.

In preparing initial drafts of many of the individual house histories, we were ably assisted by Gwen Donovan, Brooke Hyde Goode, Philip S. Kennedy-Grant, Clair Martin III, Sandy Stuart Perry, Jeanne Rice, and John Dillon Turpin. We extend our sincere appreciation to them all for taking reams of research materials and distilling that information into readable form, and for asking probing and helpful questions along the way.

Most of the more-recent photographs in the book were taken by David Gruol and the late Henry S. Fullerton III, with other photographs provided by John Dessarzin, Billy Prouty, George Peirce, Dan McCollum, David Bergeland, and Walter Choroszewski. Their work clearly confirms the adage that a picture is worth a thousand words. Digital scanning of new and archival photographs was provided by Digital Arts Imaging and the printing firm of Llewellyn & McKane. Both firms deserve kudos for cleaning up and bringing new life to many fragile and nearly lost historic images. Bradley J. Arnaud, the general manager of Llewellyn & McKane, and graphic designer Marvin Christopher Newman, deserve special recognition for the publishing expertise and helpful guidance they provided during the important early phases of this project.

Some of the many others who gave us valuable assistance included, in alphabetical order, Thomas B. Anderson, John Ansede, Angeline F. Austin, Ania Baas, James C. Brady, Russell E. Burke III, Paul S. Byard, Jacqueline Campbell, Charles M. Chapin III, Percy and Sally Chubb, John Clinedinst, Harden and Ailsa Crawford, Mimi Winston Daly, Elizabeth Hardenbergh Dillon, Sidney G. Dillon, Aleta Dinorcia, Sead Dizdarevic, Claire Eckert, Alison Pyne Ewing, Hugh H. Fenwick, Oliver D. Filley, Joan Fullerton, John H. and Suzy Gerbeth, Patricia Haines, David V. Hedley, Wayne Holman, Richard Lindabury Hull, Condict Hyde, Sylvia Talmage Kissel, Sister M. Pierre Koesters, Sarah Landau, Caroline Lareuse, William E. Lawton, Patricia Lazor, Janet S. Loengard, David W. Major, Richard Marchand, Anne Clark Martindell, Richard McGinn, Jack McNamara, Clive Meanwell, George Mosle, Henry Mottern, David Myers, Jane R. Odenweller, Philip H. Pitney, James Porter, Beth Potter, Sumner C. Putnam, Evelyn Sloane Pyne, Nancy Buck Pyne, Althea Ridley, Kathryn Rust, M. Kerby Saunders II, Reeve Schley, Sissy Schley, John Charles Smith, Clifford and Mimi Starrett, Cindy Stern, Deirdre Sullivan, Prentice Talmage, Guy Torsilieri, Talie Tuffnell, William Turnbull, Hiland Hall Turner, Alana Van Rensselaer, Robert Vernon, Peter L. Villa, Herbert and Cathy Vinnicombe, Virginia Vogel, Diana Vreeland, Ellen Vreeland, Anne Walker, Richard Widdicombe, Joseph B. Wiley Jr., and Alan Willemsen.

We are especially grateful to Mark Alan Hewitt for his introduction to this volume, his encouragement throughout the project, and for his extensive scholarship concerning the opulent country houses that were built from the late 1800s through the Great Depression and their significance in American architectural, cultural, and social history. We also thank Mark for having steered us to Thomas Whitridge, of Ink, Inc., and Antony Drobinski, of Emsworth Design, Inc., who designed this volume. We are very appreciative, not only for the talent, creativity, and sensitivity that Tom and Tony brought to the task, but also for having guided us through, and for helping to ease our anxieties during, the complex process of getting our first book printed.

Our deepest thanks are extended to our editor, Brooke Hyde Goode, for her unstinting efforts to meld the work of many into a cohesive and readable whole. Not only did Brooke bring a professional editor's eye and discipline to the task, but her deep family roots in the area—her grandfather was prominent local architect A. Musgrave Hyde and her great-grandfather was A. Fillmore Hyde, a longtime master of the Essex Fox Hounds—gave her a unique perspective that was of inestimable value.

In addition to the general dedication we made at the front of the book, Jack extends a personal dedication to his wife, Marge, for her support and forbearance over the past three years; and Barry extends his dedication to Carrère & Hastings and James Leal Greenleaf, the architects who, at *Blairsden*, created a masterpiece of design that sparked a lifelong interest in architecture.

Lastly, we must acknowledge that, although many people generously contributed their time, recollections, personal archives, and insights to this project, any mistakes or omissions are strictly our own.

PHOTOGRAPHIC CREDITS